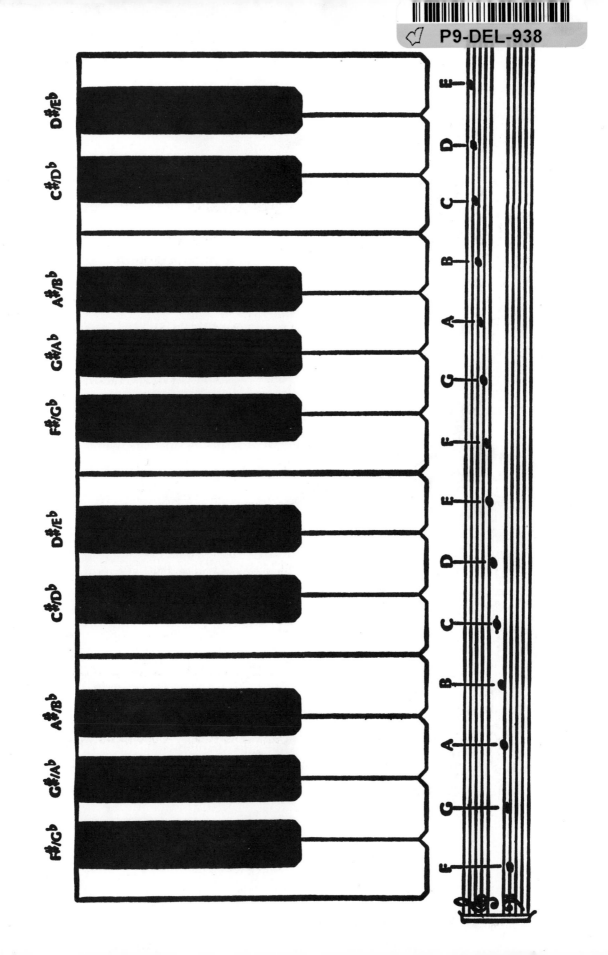

THE Music CONNECTION

SILVER BURDETT GINN

PROGRAM AUTHORS

Jane Beethoven
Dulce Bohn
Patricia Shehan Campbell
Carmen E. Culp
Jennifer Davidson
Lawrence Eisman
Sandra Longoria Glover
Charlotte Hayes

Martha Hilley
Mary E. Hoffman
Sanna Longden
Hunter March
Bill McCloud
Janet Montgomery
Marvelene Moore
Catherine Nadon-Gabrion

Mary Palmer
Carmino Ravosa
Mary Louise Reilly
Will Schmid
Carol Scott-Kassner
Jean Sinor
Sandra Stauffer
Judith Thomas

RECORDING PRODUCERS

Darrell Bledsoe
Jeanine Levenson

J. Douglas Pummill
Buryl Red, Executive Producer

Linda Twine
Ted Wilson

Scott Foresman

Editorial Offices: Glenview, IL • Parsippany, NJ • New York, NY
Sales Offices: Reading, MA • Duluth, GA • Glenview, IL
Carrollton, TX • Menlo Park, CA

ISBN 0-382-34503-7

C·O·N·T

· E · N · T · S

CONCEPTS

What is music made of?

Do you know why a dance song from Mexico sounds
different from a lullaby from China?

You'll have an opportunity to find
out when you make
the "Concept Connection."

As you sing and play and listen to the music
in this section of your book, you will
learn many things about the
basic materials of music and how they
are combined in songs and instrumental pieces.

And you'll use many
of the things you learn about
rhythm, melody, and form
in music you compose yourself.

section 1

A Song for the Children

Words by Becky and Harry Manfredini   Music by Gary Haberman   **CD 1-1, 2**

Chorus

1. This is a song for the chil - dren, The chil-dren all o - ver the world.
2. This is a song for the chil - dren, The chil-dren all o - ver the world.

From Can-a - da, Eur - ope and Mex - i - co,___ To
From In - di - a, Af - ri - ca and It - a - ly, ___ To

Rus-sia, A - mer - i-ca and To - ky-o. ___ We are the hope and the fu -
Chi-na, Aus-tral - ia and Ger-ma-ny. ___ In so man-y ways we are dif-

- ture, ___ Please give us the free - dom to grow. ___
- frent, ___ In so man-y ways we're the same. ___

Hand in hand we will learn to - day, ___ Hand in hand we will work
Hand in hand we will cel - e - brate, ___ Hand in hand we'll com-mu -

HELLO

_ and play, _
- ni - cate,
}
Mak-ing new friends _ wher-ev-er we may go, _ We

start out by say - ing "hel-lo." _

Echo

Hel - lo   Bon-jour   Sha-lom, Ni-how

Hel - lo   Bue-nos dí-as   Yai-sou, Jam-bo

Hel - lo   Gu-ten Tag   Bu - na, A-lo _

Solo

Hav-ing new friends _ can be _ Like liv-ing in one great big fam-i-ly, _

Chorus

A fam-'ly of chil-dren, We start out by say - ing "hel-lo." _

Feel the Beat...

Jumpin' out of bed...

Have you ever had a morning when everything seemed to go wrong — a morning like the one described in this song?

Follow the words as you listen to the recording and join in on the refrain.

I'm Not Gonna Let That Ruin My Day   CD 1-3

Words by Wes Caswell   Music by Cici Hunt

C   F

1. Woke up this morn - in' _____ rar - in' to go. ____
2. On my way to break - fast, _____ stum-bled on a rug.
3. On my way to _____ school, __ go - in' out the door.
4. Sit - tin' down to lunch _ in my brand new _ shirt, __ Saw a

C   G7

Jump - in' out of bed, I stubbed my toe. _____
Fly - ing through the air, I swal - lowed a bug, _____
Heard my kid sis - ter let out a roar, __ She
pret - ty _____ girl, __ she be - gan to flirt. _____

C   F

Hop - pin' a - round __ with one foot in the air, _____
Land - ed in the kit - chen, _ flat on my back. ___
hol - lered at me, _____ said I was dumb, __
Mus - tard for my hot dog, ___ ket - chup for my fries,

ROCK 'N' ROLL

Rock Around the Clock

Words and Music by M. Freedman and J. Deknight

CD 1-4

INTRODUCTION

One, two, three - o' - clock, four o' - clock rock!

Five, six, sev - en o'-clock, eight o' - clock rock!

Nine, ten, e - lev - en o'-clock, twelve o' - clock rock!

We're gon - na rock a - round the clock to - night!

Like all rock songs, this popular song of the 1950s has a strong, steady beat. Find a way to show the steady beat as you listen to the music. The headline at the top of the page may give you an idea.

Elvis Presley is remembered as the king of rock and roll. Here is one of the songs that he made famous.

Blue Suede Shoes
................Carl Lee Perkins

CD 1-5

1. Put your glad rags on, join me hon', we'll have some fun when the clock strikes one,
We're gonna rock around the clock tonight, we're gonna rock, rock, rock 'til the broad daylight,
We're gonna rock, we're gonna rock around the clock tonight.

2. When the clock strikes two, three and four, if the band slows down, we'll yell for more,
We're gonna rock around the clock tonight, we're gonna rock, rock, rock 'til the broad daylight,
We're gonna rock, we're gonna rock around the clock tonight.

3. When the chimes ring five, six and seven, we'll be right in seventh heav'n,
We're gonna rock around the clock tonight, we're gonna rock, rock, rock 'til the broad daylight,
We're gonna rock, we're gonna rock around the clock tonight.

4. When it's eight, nine, ten, eleven, too, I'll be goin' strong and so will you,
We're gonna rock around the clock tonight, we're gonna rock, rock, rock, 'til the broad daylight,
We're gonna rock, we're gonna rock around the clock tonight.

Instrumental interlude

5. When the clock strikes twelve, we'll cool off.
Then start-a rockin' round the clock again,
We're gonna rock around the clock tonight, we're gonna rock, rock, rock, 'til the broad daylight,
We're gonna rock, we're gonna rock around the clock tonight.

KEEP

A well-known recording group called Sweet Honey in the Rock tells the story of *The Little Shekere.* As you listen to the recording, snap, tap, or clap the beat, following the words below.

CD 1-6

The Little Shekere .... Nitanju Bolade Casel

The Little Shekere

I used to be a squash in Aminatta's field
Until the day she decided to collect her yield.
I was so afraid she would come and choose me,
but since I couldn't run away, I had to wait and see.

She went back and forth and up and down every row,
Then without choosing me she decided to go.
I was so relieved I began to shout!
Which made her turn around and see me so she picked me out.

When she wrapped me in her sack and placed me on her head
And started walking to the village, I was filled with dread.
Many of my friends and family had left the land,
But never knowing where they went I did not understand.

That a whole new life was just ahead for me
as a calabash, *moraccas, agbe,* or *axatse.*
I never knew a squash could be so many things,
Full of colors and designs and beaded down with strings.

When we reached the house they took me out of the sack.
I wanted to go home! Somebody take me back!
But as I looked around I just could not believe my eyes.
I saw my friends and family, what a nice surprise!

They were happy to see me and they were looking good
And when they started to talk that's when I understood.
Even though each one was different in color and shape,
When they all played together the music was great.

My life was just beginning in the musical world,
I'd be a shekere for these young boys and girls.
A Shekere! A Shekere! A Shekere! A Shekere!
So listen everybody to my family and friends,
We're gonna sing this song for you from beginning to end.
A Shekere! A Shekere! A Shekere! A Shekere!

THE BEAT

Sweet Honey
in the Rock

Steady Silent BEAT

You will hear a recording of a song called *Rag Mop*. To help you feel the steady beat, perform the pattern below by making the PAT-clap motions and chanting the words softly.

PAT– clap, PAT– clap, PAT – clap, PAT – clap

 Rag Mop ....Wills and Anderson

CD 1-7

Rhythm Game

Look at the four-measure patterns below. Each number represents one beat. Chant the numbers aloud and clap only those beats that are circled.

1. ①②③④ | ①②③④ | ①②③④ | ①②③④ |

2. ①②③ 4 | ①②③ 4 | ①②③ 4 | ①②③ 4 |

3. ① 2 ③④ | ① 2 ③④ | ① 2 ③④ | ① 2 ③④ |

4. ① 2 3 ④ | ① 2 3 ④ | ① 2 3 ④ | ① 2 3 ④ |

5. ① 2 3 ④ | ①② 3 ④ | 1 ②③ 4 | 1 ② 3 ④ |

6. ①②③④ | 1 2 3 4 | ①②③④ | 1 2 3 ④ |

When you perform the patterns again, just *think* the numbers and clap the circled beats. The uncircled numbers represent **rests**, or silent beats.

Follow the music as you listen to the recording of "Joe Turner Blues." Pay particular attention to the "breaks" (rests) in the melody at the end of each line.

Joe Turner Blues   CD 1-8

Blues Song from the United States

1. They tell me — Joe Turn-er's — come and gone, —
2. He came here — with for - ty — links of chain, —
3. Joe Turn-er, — he took my — man a - way, —

They tell me — Joe Turn-er's — come and gone. —
He came here — with for - ty — links of chain. —
Joe Turn-er, — he took my — man a - way, —

He left me — here to sing —— this —— song.

Listen to another version of *Joe Turner Blues*. Listen especially for the voice part. What do you hear?

Joe Turner Blues, Version 2
............Blues Song from the United States

CD 1-9

The BEAT GOES ON

Breathe Easy Blues   CD 1-10

Words and Music by Gene Grier and Lowell Everson

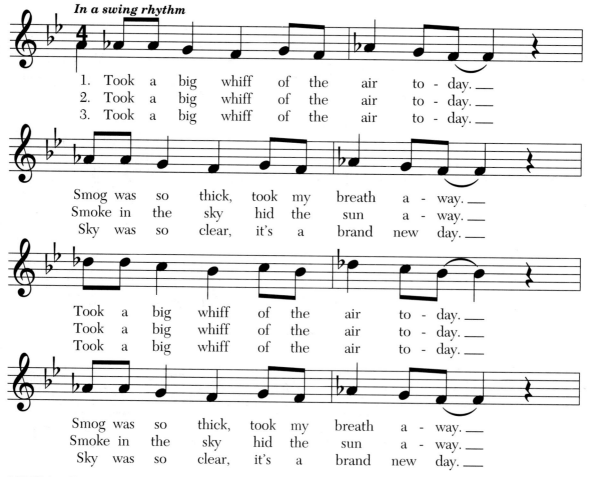

In a swing rhythm

1. Took a big whiff of the air to - day. __
2. Took a big whiff of the air to - day. __
3. Took a big whiff of the air to - day. __

Smog was so thick, took my breath a - way. __
Smoke in the sky hid the sun a - way. __
Sky was so clear, it's a brand new day. __

Took a big whiff of the air to - day. __
Took a big whiff of the air to - day. __
Took a big whiff of the air to - day. __

Smog was so thick, took my breath a - way. __
Smoke in the sky hid the sun a - way. __
Sky was so clear, it's a brand new day. __

Keep the beat by snapping one of these patterns as you listen to the recording of "Breathe Easy Blues." Keep the pattern going all through the song.

1.

2.

3.

1.,2.

Got to pay our _ dues, _ or get the breathe eas-y blues. _

3.

Got to pay our _ dues, _ up to us to __ choose. _

We can win, then _ lose __ those smell-y breathe eas - y blues, _

those smell-y breathe eas-y blues, _ those smell-y breathe eas-y blues. _

CLOCK MUSIC

"Viennese Musical Clock" is the second movement of a suite called *Háry János,* adapted from the opera of the same name by its composer, Zoltán Kodály.

Háry János is a well-known figure in Hungarian folklore. He is an old soldier who tells tall tales so well that everyone believes they are true. One of Háry János' stories is about his trip to Vienna where he saw the great musical clock of the Imperial Palace. In "Viennese Musical Clock," Kodály paints a musical picture of the mechanical figures that parade around the palace clock on the stroke of every hour.

"Viennese Musical Clock" from *Háry János*
.....................*Zoltán Kodály*

CD 1-11

Leroy Anderson, an American composer, wrote a short piece for orchestra called *Syncopated Clock*. What happens to the sound of the clock in this piece?

Syncopated Clock...............
Leroy Anderson

CD 1-12

Persistence of Memory   *Salvador Dali*

Move to the BEAT

Some older popular songs have lots of nonsense words. They help to keep the rhythm going. Try "poppin'" your fingers and "shufflin'" your feet in time to the music as you listen to the recording of "Do Wah Diddy Diddy."

Snap-Clap Hand Pattern

Perform this hand pattern as you sing "Do Wah Diddy Diddy" with the recording. Notice the rest at the end of the pattern.

(snap)   (clap)

Use the snap-clap pattern to keep time to the music of this merry dance tune.

🎧 "Polka" from *Schwanda, the Bagpiper*
..................Jaromír Weinberger
CD 1-16

Do Wah Diddy Diddy (excerpt)

CD 1-14, 15

Words and Music by Jeff Barry and Ellie Greenwich

There he was ___ just a - walk - in' down the street,
fore I knew it he was walk - in' next to me,

Sing - in' Do wah did - dy did-dy down did-dy do, Pop - pin' his fin - gers and a -
Took ___ my hand ___ just as

shuf - fl - in' his feet, Sing - in' Do wah did - dy did - dy
nat - ural as can be,

down did - dy do. He looked good, (yeah, yeah) He looked
We walked on, (yeah, yeah) To my

fine, (yeah, yeah) He looked good, he looked fine, and I
door, (yeah, yeah) We walked on to my door, and he

1.
near - ly lost my mind.

2.
Be - stayed a lit - tle more, Sing - in'

Do wah did - dy did - dy down did - dy do.

SETS OF TWO

The chariot described in this African American spiritual is bound for heaven.

Find a way to keep the steady beat as you listen to the recording of this joyful song.

Gonna Ride Up in the Chariot   CD 1-17

African American Spiritual

VERSE D   G   A

1. Gon-na ride up in the char-iot, Soon-a in the morn-in',

D   G   D

Ride up in the char-iot, Soon-a in the morn-in', Ride up in the char-iot,

G   A   D   A₇   D

Soon-a in the morn-in', And I hope I'll join the band.

REFRAIN D   G   A₇

O, Lord, have mer-cy on me, O, Lord, have mer-cy on me,

Can you find these rhythm patterns in the song? Clap the patterns and then play them on a percussion instrument. Which instrument will you choose?

1.
2.
3.
4.

O, Lord, have mer - cy on me,

And I hope I'll join the band.

2. Gonna meet my brother there, yes, Soon-a in the morn-in',
   Meet my brother there, yes, Soon-a in the morn-in',
   Meet my brother there, yes, Soon-a in the morn-in',
   And I hope I'll join the band. *Refrain*

3. Gonna chatter with the angels, Soon-a in the morn-in',
   Chatter with the angels, Soon-a in the morn-in',
   Chatter with the angels, Soon-a in the morn-in',
   And I hope I'll join the band. *Refrain*

METER in 2

Feel the beats moving in sets of two as you listen to the recording of this traditional song from Texas.

The Yellow Rose of Texas

CD 1-18, 19

Traditional

1. There's a yel-low rose in Tex-as That I am going to see.
2. Oh, I'm go-ing back to find her, My heart is full of woe.

No oth-er fel-low knows her, No-bod-y else but me.
We'll sing the songs to-geth-er We sang so long a-go.

She cried so when I left her, It al-most broke my heart,
I'll pick the ban-jo gai-ly, And sing the songs of yore.

And if I ev-er find her, we nev-er more shall part.
The Yel-low Rose of Tex-as, She'll be mine for-ev-er more.

Play a Part

The number in the color box in each pattern below tells you how many beats there are in each measure. Play one of these percussion parts to accompany "The Yellow Rose of Texas." Which part will you choose? Which percussion instrument will you use?

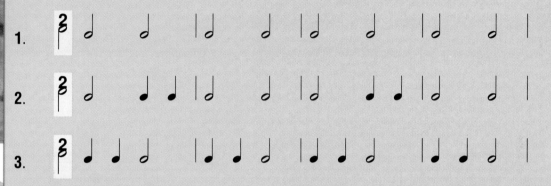

1.
2.
3.

As you listen to the recording of *Cripple Creek,* decide whether the beats are grouped in twos or in threes. Make up a hand pattern that will show what you hear.

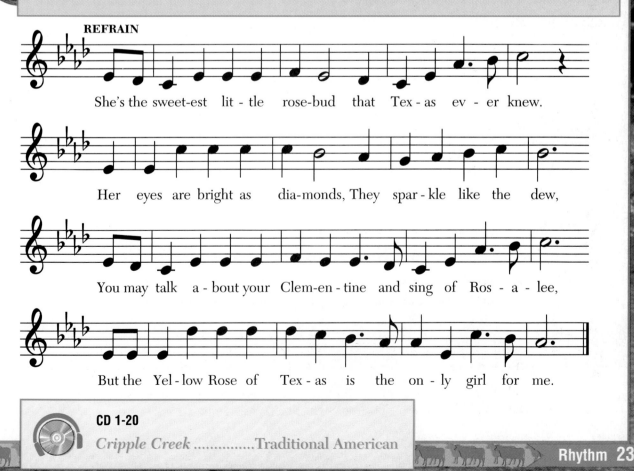

REFRAIN

She's the sweet-est lit - tle rose-bud that Tex - as ev - er knew.

Her eyes are bright as dia-monds, They spar - kle like the dew,

You may talk a - bout your Clem-en - tine and sing of Ros - a - lee,

But the Yel - low Rose of Tex - as is the on - ly girl for me.

CD 1-20

Cripple Creek ....Traditional American

METER IN 3

Pat the steady beat on your knees as you listen to this folk song from Austria.

Cuckoo CD 1-21

English Words by Katherine F. Rohrbough   *Folk Song from Austria*

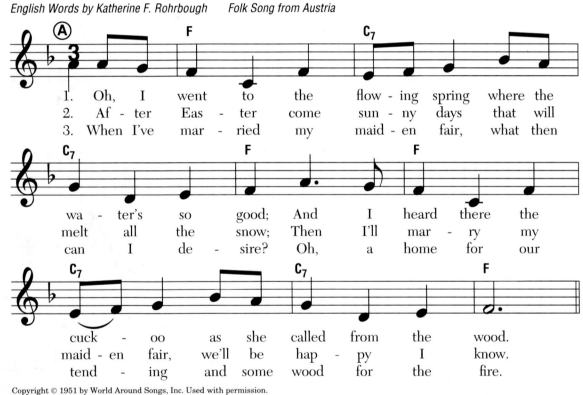

1. Oh, I went to the flow - ing spring where the
2. Af - ter Eas - ter come sun - ny days that will
3. When I've mar - ried my maid - en fair, what then

wa - ter's so good; And I heard there the
melt all the snow; Then I'll mar - ry my
can I de - sire? Oh, a home for our

cuck - oo as she called from the wood.
maid - en fair, we'll be hap - py I know.
tend - ing and some wood for the fire.

REFRAN

B C₇   F

Hoh - lee - ah,   Hoh - leh - rah - hee - hee - ah,

C₇   C₇

Hoh - leh - rah   cuck - oo.   Hoh - leh - rah - hee - hee - ah,

F   F

Hoh - leh - rah   cuck - oo.   Hoh - leh - rah - hee - hee - ah,

C₇   C₇   F

Hoh - leh-rah   cuck - oo,   Hoh - leh-rah - hee - hee - ah - hoh.

Perform the pat-clap-snap hand pattern as you listen to this recording.

CD 1-22

American Children .... Black and Bialek

2'S OR 3'S

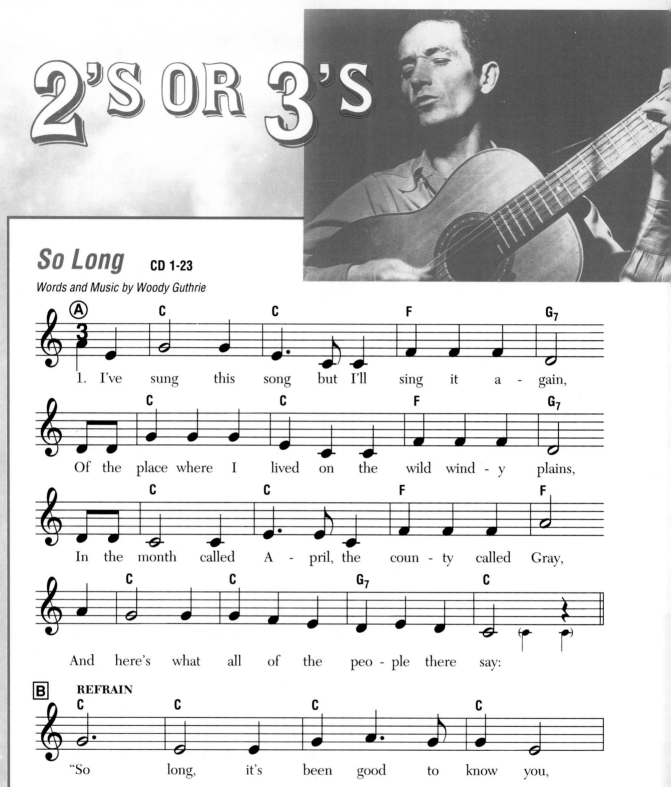

So Long   CD 1-23

Words and Music by Woody Guthrie

A

C / C / F / G7

1. I've sung this song but I'll sing it a - gain,

C / C / F / G7

Of the place where I lived on the wild wind - y plains,

C / C / F / F

In the month called A - pril, the coun - ty called Gray,

C / C / G7 / C

And here's what all of the peo - ple there say:

B **REFRAIN**

C / C / C / C

"So long, it's been good to know you,

Woody Guthrie composed more than 1000 songs that tell about people and their ways of living. In this song, Woody tells about the time when most of the Southwest was turned into a "dust bowl."

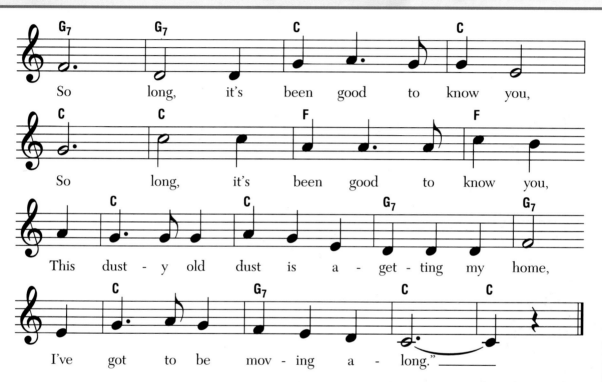

So long, it's been good to know you,

So long, it's been good to know you,

This dust-y old dust is a-get-ting my home,

I've got to be mov-ing a-long."

2. A dust storm hit and it hit like thunder,
   It dusted us over and covered us under,
   It blocked out the traffic and blocked out the sun,
   And straight for home all the people did run, singing:
   Refrain

3. We talked of the end of the world, and then
   We'd sing a song, and then sing it again.
   We'd set for an hour and not say a word,
   And then these words would be heard:
   Refrain

Make up a hand pattern that will show what you hear.

"Minuet" from Notebook for Anna Magdalena Bach ....Johann S. Bach

CD 1-24

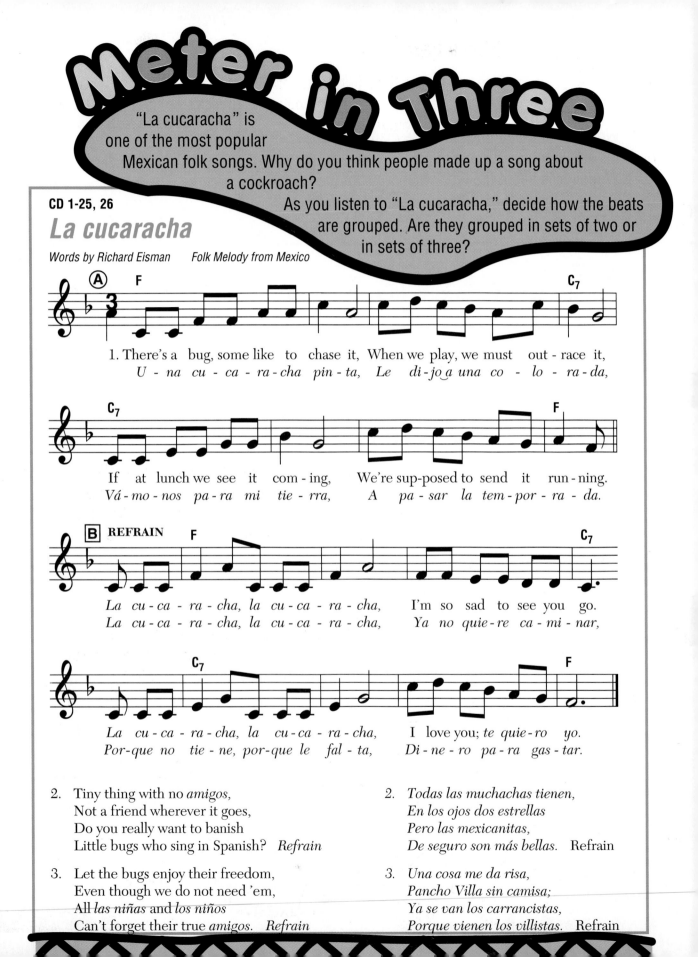

Meter in Three

"La cucaracha" is one of the most popular Mexican folk songs. Why do you think people made up a song about a cockroach?

As you listen to "La cucaracha," decide how the beats are grouped. Are they grouped in sets of two or in sets of three?

CD 1-25, 26

La cucaracha

Words by Richard Eisman   Folk Melody from Mexico

Ⓐ

1. There's a bug, some like to chase it, When we play, we must out-race it,
U - na cu - ca - ra - cha pin - ta, Le di-jo a una co - lo - ra - da,

If at lunch we see it com - ing, We're sup-posed to send it run - ning.
Vá - mo - nos pa - ra mi tie - rra, A pa - sar la tem - por - ra - da.

Ⓑ REFRAIN

La cu - ca - ra - cha, la cu - ca - ra - cha, I'm so sad to see you go.
La cu - ca - ra - cha, la cu - ca - ra - cha, Ya no quie - re ca - mi - nar,

La cu - ca - ra - cha, la cu - ca - ra - cha, I love you; *te quie - ro yo.*
Por-que no tie - ne, por-que le fal - ta, Di - ne - ro pa - ra gas - tar.

2. Tiny thing with no *amigos*,
   Not a friend wherever it goes,
   Do you really want to banish
   Little bugs who sing in Spanish?   *Refrain*

3. Let the bugs enjoy their freedom,
   Even though we do not need 'em,
   All *las niñas* and *los niños*
   Can't forget their true *amigos.*   *Refrain*

2. *Todas las muchachas tienen,*
   En los ojos dos estrellas
   Pero las mexicanitas,
   De seguro son más bellas.   Refrain

3. *Una cosa me da risa,*
   Pancho Villa sin camisa;
   Ya se van los carrancistas,
   Porque vienen los villistas.   Refrain

Play a Part

The number in the color box in each pattern below tells you how many beats there are in each measure. Choose one of the patterns to play on a percussion instrument to accompany the song.

Follow the chord names in the music and play this pattern on the autoharp.

As you listen to this popular Mexican folk song, decide whether the music moves along in a meter of 2 or in a meter of 3. Make up a hand pattern that will show what you hear.

Cuatro milpas.....................Folk
Song from Mexico

CD 1-27

Here is a famous Mexican song that has changing meter. Can you hear when the music changes from meter in 2 to meter in 3?

Jarabe tapatio ....Folk
Song from Mexico

CD 1-28

Royal Fireworks

George Frideric Handel composed *Royal Fireworks Music* for an outdoor spectacle including fireworks and a 101- cannon salute.

You will hear two pieces from *Royal Fireworks Music*. The title of each piece is the name of an old dance.

ABOUT THE COMPOSER

George Frideric Handel   (1685-1759)

George Frideric Handel was born in the small German city of Halle in 1685. When he was still a child, Handel decided that he would be a musician when he grew up. But his father had other plans. He wanted his son to become a lawyer.

At first, Handel's father (who didn't think much of music) ordered George to give up the notion of becoming a musician. But later on he recognized his son's musical gifts and arranged for George to have the finest music teachers.

During his lifetime, Handel spent a lot of time traveling from one country to another. He finally settled in England, where he composed many pieces, including *Royal Fireworks Music*, that are still favorites with concert audiences all over the world.

Here is the first theme of "Bourrée." What sign in the music tells you the piece is in meter in 2?

Here is the first theme of "Minuet." What sign in the music tells you the piece is in meter in 3?

"Bourrée" and "Minuet"
from *Royal Fireworks Music*
CD 1-30, 31 ....George Frideric Handel

MELODY a line of sound

Fifty-Ninth Street Bridge Song (Feelin' Groovy)

Words and Music by Paul Simon **CD 2-2, 3**

Slow down, _ you move too fast. _ You got to make the morn-

- ing last. _ Just kick-in' down the cob-ble-stones, _

look-in' for fun and feel - in' groov - y. _____

Hel-lo lamp-post, what-cha know-in'? I've come to watch your flow-

- ers grow - in' Ain't-cha got no rhymes _ for me?

Doot-in' doo-doo, feel-in' groov - y. _____ Got

no deeds to do, no prom-is - es to keep. I'm dap-pled and drow-sy and

read - y   to sleep. Let the   morn-ing-time drop all   its   pet - als   on   me.

Life,   I   love   you,   All   is groov - y. _____

The Brooklyn Bridge: Variation on an Old Theme, 1939
Joseph Stella

Follow the rise and fall of the melody line as you listen to this song.

How does the artist, Joseph Stella, use lines in this painting of the Brooklyn Bridge?

TONES CAN REPEAT

Follow the music as you listen to the recording of "The M.T.A. Song." Can you find places in the melody where the tones repeat?

The M.T.A. Song   CD 2-4

Words and Music by Jacqueline Steiner and Bess Hawes

1. Well let me tell you of the sto - ry of the man named Char-lie,
2. Char - lie hand-ed in his dime __ at the Kendall Square Sta-tion,
3. Now __ all __ night __ long __ Char-lie rides through the tun-nel,

On a trag - ic and fate - ful day. _____
And he changed for Ja - mai - ca Plain. _____
Say - ing, "What will be - come of me? _____

He put ten cents in his pock - et, kissed his wife and fam - 'ly,
When he got there, the con - duc - tor told him one more nick - el,
How can I af - ford to see __ my __ sister in Chel - sea,

went to ride on the M. T. A.
Char - lie could - n't get off the train.
Or my cous - in in Rox - bur - y?"

KENDALL SQUARE

Listen for many **repeated tones** in these two very different pieces.

Poverty Knock
...........English Work Song
CD 2-5

Symphony No. 7, Movement 2
...........Ludwig van Beethoven
CD 2-6

REFRAIN

1.-4. Well did he ev-er re-turn? _ No, he nev-er re-turned, _
5. Or else he'll nev-er re-turn. _ No, he'll nev-er re-turn, __

And his fate is still un - learned. _____ He may
And his fate will be un - learned. _____ He may

ride for - ev-er 'neath the streets of Bos - ton,
ride for - ev-er 'neath the streets of Bos - ton.

He's the man who nev-er re - turned.
He's the man who nev-er re - turned.

4. Charlie's wife goes down to the Scollay Square Station,
Ev'ry day at quarter past two.
And through the open window she hands Charlie a sandwich,
As the train comes rumblin' through. *Refrain*

5. Now, you citizens of Boston, don't you think it is a scandal,
That the people have to pay and pay?
Fight the fare increase, Fight the fare increase,
Get Charlie off the M.T.A. *Refrain*

Upward and Downward

Find the two color boxes in the notation of this song. How do the notes move in each color box?

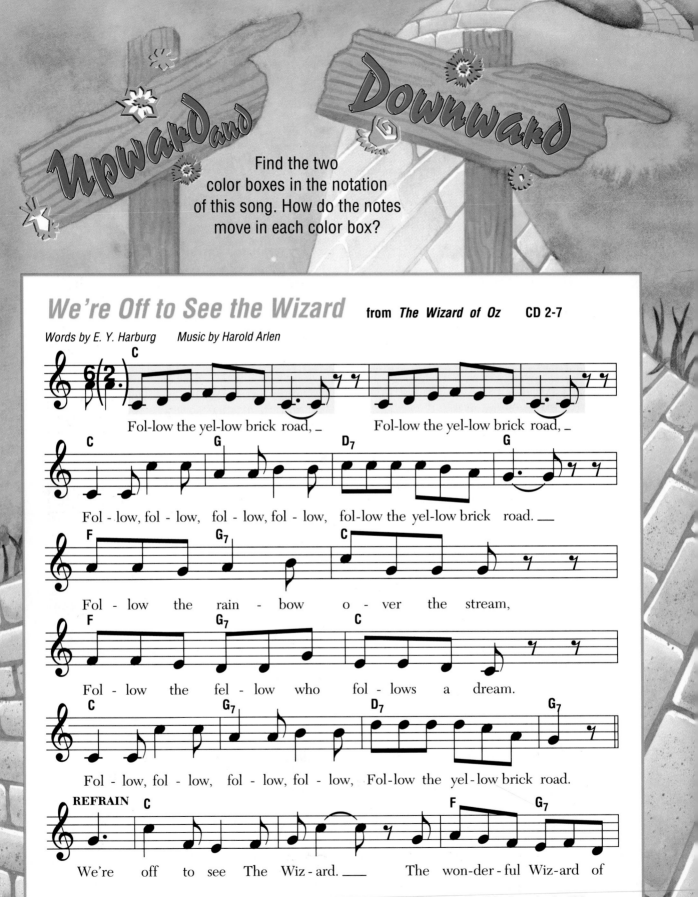

We're Off to See the Wizard

from *The Wizard of Oz* CD 2-7

Words by E. Y. Harburg   Music by Harold Arlen

Fol-low the yel-low brick road, _ Fol-low the yel-low brick road, _

Fol - low, fol - low, fol - low, fol - low, fol-low the yel-low brick road. __

Fol - low the rain - bow o - ver the stream,

Fol - low the fel - low who fol - lows a dream.

Fol - low, fol - low, fol - low, fol - low, Fol-low the yel - low brick road.

REFRAIN

We're off to see The Wiz - ard. ___ The won-der-ful Wiz-ard of

Oz. _____ We hear he is a whiz of a wiz if
ev - er a wiz there was. _____ If ev - er, oh, ev - er a
wiz there was, The Wiz - ard of Oz is one be - coz, be -
coz, be - coz, be - coz, be - coz, be - coz, _____ Be -
coz of the won - der - ful things he does. We're
off to see the Wiz-ard, __ The won-der-ful Wiz-ard of Oz. __

As you listen to the recording of "Over the Rainbow," follow the music and notice the color boxes. How do the tones move in the red color boxes? How do the tones move in the blue color boxes?

Over the Rainbow

from *The Wizard of Oz*   CD 2-9

Words by E. Y. Harburg   Music by Harold Arlen

Some - where   o - ver the rain - bow,   way   up   high,

There's   a   land that I heard of   once   in a lull - a - by.

Some - where   o - ver the rain - bow   skies   are   blue,

And   the   dreams that you dare to   dream real - ly do come true.

Some - day I'll wish up - on   a   star and   wake up where the clouds are   far   be -

"We're Off to See the Wizard" (page 36 in your book) and "Over the Rainbow" are songs from the popular movie *The Wizard of Oz*. Here is another song from the same movie.

 "If I Only Had a Brain" from *The Wizard of Oz*
.................E. Y. Harburg and Harold Arlen

CD 2-10

hind me; _____ Where trou-bles melt like lem-on drops, a-

way, a-bove the chim-ney tops, that's where you'll find me.

Some-where o-ver the rain-bow blue-birds fly,

Birds fly o-ver the rain-bow, why, then, oh why, can't

I? If hap-py lit-tle blue-birds fly be-

yond the rain-bow, why, oh why, can't I? _____

Rain Song CD 2-11

Words and Music by David McHugh

The rain just keeps on fall-ing, And the sky is col-ored grey;

The birds don't stop their sing-ing __ 'Cause it's just an-oth-er day;

And the clouds keep pass-ing o - ver, Bring-in' rain to flow'rs be - low;

While the sun keeps wait-ing pa-tient-ly To un - veil its gold-en glow;

Some-times sun shines, and oth - er times it rains; _____

But to me it's all the same, _____

To me it's all the same. _____

© 1972 David McHugh. Shadow Canyon Music. Used by permission.

Notice how the composer uses repeated tones in "Rain Song."

Listen for repeated tones in a piano piece by Frédéric Chopin.

Prelude in D Flat (" The Raindrop")
.....................Frédéric Chopin
CD 2-12

MEET THE COMPOSER

On the recording of "Rain Song," the composer David McHugh sings the song and accompanies himself at the piano. On this recording, Mr. McHugh talks about his career in music and plays some music from his movie score *Moscow on the Hudson.*

CD 2-13
Careers in Music—David McHugh

STEPS LEAPS and REPEATS

Listen for steps, leaps, and repeats in this dance for symphony orchestra.

"Gavotte" from *Classical Symphony*
...................Sergei Prokofiev

CD 2-16

That's How I'd Be Without You

Words by Wes Caswell   Music by Cici Hunt   **CD 2-15**

1. Like a church with-out a steep-le, Like a lamp with-out a shade.
   rod with-out a reel,__ Like a rose with-out a bud.
   Min - nie and__ Mick-ey, Tar - zan__ and Jane.
   sail with-out a boat.__ Like a bird with-out a beak.

Like a mall with-out the peo - ple, Like a skate with-out a blade.
Like a shoe with-out a heel,__ Like a cow with-out a cud.
Ro - me - o and Ju - li - et__ top - hat__ and cane.
Like a song with-out a note.__ Like a hide with-out a seek.

Like a   car with-out   a horn. Like a   sleuth with-out   a clue.
Like an   owl with-out   a hoot, Like a   ghost with-out   a "boo."
Ba - con and __ eggs,   hot __   fudge and   ice __   cream.
Like a   night with-out   a star. Like a   dove with-out   a "coo."

1.
2.

That's how I'd be with-out   you.   2. Like a   you.
That's how I'd be with-out
We __ make a great

3.
team,   yeah.   We make _ a great   team!

REFRAIN

We go to-geth-er, _   Birds of a feath-er. _   We're like peach-es and cream.

Like the   Gi-ants and the Yank-ees. The   "hank-y's" and the "pank-y's," _

D.S.

We   make _ a great   team.

3. We're
4. Like a

𝄉 *Coda*

That's how I'd be with-out   you,   yeah,   That's how I'd be with-out   you.

Melody 43

A ONE-ACT OPERA

Amahl and the Night Visitors by Gian Carlo Menotti was the first opera written especially for television. The first performance was given on Christmas Eve, 1951. The Night Visitors in the opera were the Three Kings who Menotti remembered from his childhood in Italy. It was the Three Kings who brought gifts to the children at Christmas time. Menotti has called this opera an "opera for children."

Menotti calls "Shepherd's Dance" a kind of neighborhood welcome or greeting to the Three Kings. Follow the chart as you listen to the music.

CD 2-17

"Shepherd's Dance" from *Amahl and the Night Visitors*
Gian Carlo Menotti

Introduction

String bass and cello play a short pattern softly and slowly.

Section A

The string bass and cello pattern continue as two oboes play follow-the-leader.

At times the oboes play together.

The oboe duet turns into a musical contest as the tempo gets faster and faster.

Section B

Suddenly the whole orchestra breaks into a fast-moving dance playing three different tunes, heard one after the other.

The music becomes more and more spirited and the exciting dance comes to an end with a loud fanfare of repeated tones.

A Pattern That Repeats

As you listen to the recording of "Happiness Runs," draw a circle in the air for each two-measure phrase.

Add a Harmony Part

You can add harmony by playing the autoharp chords as the class sings the song. What can you discover about the chord pattern in each phrase?

Another way to add harmony to a song is to play or sing an ostinato—a melody pattern that repeats. Perform one of these ostinatos as the class sings the song.

1.
Pa - pa - pa - pa

2.

3.

Happiness Runs

CD 2-19

Traditional

A Hap - pi - ness runs in a cir - cu - lar mo - tion.

Love is a lit - tle boat up - on the sea.

Ev - 'ry - one is a part of ev - 'ry - thing an - y - way,

You can be hap - py if you let your - self be.

B Pa - pa - pa - pa - pa - pa - pa - pa - pa - pa - pa;

Pa - pa - pa - pa - pa - pa - pa - pa - pa;

Pa - pa - pa - pa - pa - pa - pa - pa - pa - pa - pa;

Pa - pa - pa - pa - pa - pa - pa - pa - pa.

Echo Song

Have you ever heard your own echo? Where? Try different ways of being someone else's echo.

Listen for the echo part in the recording of this song about a little bug who is looking for a home. Join in on the echo part in the refrain.

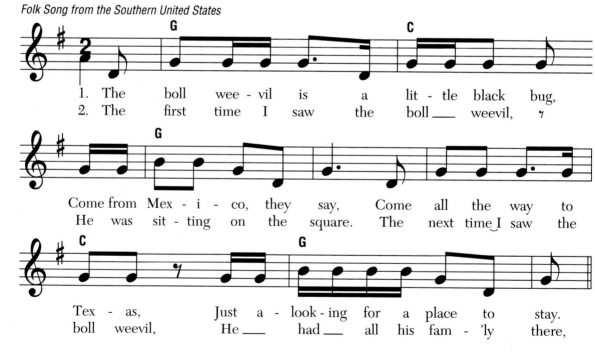

Ballad of the Boll Weevil

CD 2-20

Folk Song from the Southern United States

1. The boll wee-vil is a lit-tle black bug,
2. The first time I saw the boll ___ weevil,

Come from Mex-i-co, they say, Come all the way to
He was sit-ting on the square. The next time I saw the

Tex-as, Just a-look-ing for a place to stay.
boll weevil, He ___ had ___ all his fam-'ly there,

Pick a Percussion Part

You can use one of these parts to accompany "Ballad of the Boll Weevil."
Which one will you choose?

3. The farmer took the boll weevil
   And he put him in hot sand.
   The boll weevil said, "This is mighty hot,
   But I'll stand it like a man,
   This'll be my home, . . ."

4. The farmer took the boll weevil,
   And he put him on a lump of ice.
   The weevil said to the farmer,
   "This is mighty cool and nice,
   This'll be my home, . . ."

5. The merchant got half the cotton,
   The boll weevil got the rest;
   Didn't leave the farmer's wife
   But one old cotton dress,
   And it's full of holes, . . .

6. The farmer said to his missus,
   "Now what do you think of that?
   The boll weevil has made a nest
   In my best Sunday hat,
   He's got a home, . . ."

PARTNER SONGS

When you and your classmates can sing the songs on these two pages, you will be ready to create harmony by singing both songs at the same time.

Pick a Little, Talk a Little

from *The Music Man*   CD 2-21, 23

Words and Music by Meredith Willson

Pick a lit-tle, talk a lit-tle, pick a lit-tle, talk a lit-tle,

Cheep, cheep, cheep, talk a lot, pick a lit-tle more.

Pick a lit-tle, talk a lit-tle, pick a lit-tle, talk a lit-tle,

Cheep, cheep, cheep, talk a lot, pick a lit-tle more.

Pick a lit-tle, talk a lit-tle, pick a lit-tle, talk a lit-tle,

Cheep, cheep, cheep, talk a lot, pick a lit-tle more.

Listen to another pair of partner songs from *The Music Man*. A men's group sings one song and a woman sings the other song. Who sings the "Lida Rose" part?

"Lida Rose" and "Will I Ever Tell You?" from
The Music Man ....Meredith Willson

CD 2-24

Pick a lit - tle, talk a lit - tle, pick a lit - tle, talk a lit - tle,

Cheep, cheep, cheep, cheep, cheep, cheep, cheep, cheep,

Cheep, cheep, cheep, cheep, cheep, cheep, cheep, cheep, cheep, cheep, cheep.

Goodnight, Ladies   CD 2-22, 23

Traditional Song from the United States

Good - night, la - dies, _____ Good - night, la - dies, _____

Good - night, la - dies, _____ We're go - ing to leave you now. _____

Sleep tight.

Follow the

Can you hear voices playing follow-the-leader in the recording of "Follow Me"?

Follow Me   CD 2-25

Traditional

Come a - long. Sing a song,

Fol - low me; It is eas - y as you

see. Ev - 'ry day, In this way, Just re -

peat Till the tune's com - plete. _____

Two instruments play follow-the-leader in this listening selection. Which instrument plays first?

Sonata for Violin and Piano, Movement 4
...................César Franck

CD 2-26

Rhythm Rounds

I   II

When you're feelin' kind of blue,

There is just one thing to do.

Play that music and feel that beat;

Snap your fingers and shuffle your feet.

When you can clap the patterns notated below, team up with a friend and try clapping each pattern as a two-part round.

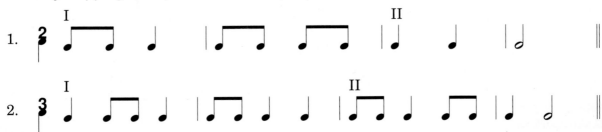

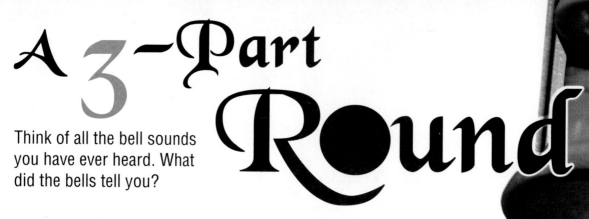

A 3-Part Round

Think of all the bell sounds you have ever heard. What did the bells tell you?

What kind of bells play the melody in the recording of this song?

The Carillon (Le Carillon) CD 2-27

Traditional Round

I F ... II

Oh, hear the ring - ing car - il - lon,
En - ten - dez vous le car - il - lon,

F ... III

Di - ri don, don, don, don, don, don, don, don, don, don.
Di - ri don, don, don, don, don, don, don, don, don, don.

Ostinatos to Sing and Play

For a special performance of "The Carillon," add an ostinato. Which of these ostinatos will you choose to accompany the song? Will you sing it? Play it on bells?

Bells or voices

Don, don, don, don.

Bells or voices

Don, don, don, don, don.

Bells in Poetry and Song

The history of bells is full of poetry and song. After hearing the sound of church bells through his open window, Edgar Allan Poe, one of America's greatest storytellers, wrote a long poem called *The Bells*. Here is the first verse of the poem. Try reading it aloud.

The Bells

Hear the sledges with the bells,
Silver bells!
What a world of merriment their
melody foretells!
How they tinkle, tinkle, tinkle,
in the icy air of night!
While the stars, that oversprinkle
All the heavens, seem to twinkle
With a crystalline delight;
Keeping time, time, time;
In a sort of runic rime,
To the tintinabulation that so musically wells
From the bells, bells, bells—
From the jingling and the tinkling of the bells.

Write your own poem about bells. Then try creating a melody that will fit your words, using the notes of the five-tone scale pictured at the left.

When you are ready, share your song with the class.

Music for a Village Celebration

Georges Bizet composed a group of pieces to accompany a play called *L'Arlésienne*—"The Woman of Arles." The *Carillon*, or bell music, introduces the fourth scene of the drama. The courtyard is decorated with garlands of poppies and cornflowers and the village people have gathered to celebrate the feast of Saint Eloi, patron of farm folk. They are also celebrating the coming wedding of their young friends Frédéri and Vivette.

Three Themes

Pretend you are one of the villagers as you follow the chart and listen to the music of *Carillon*.

L'Arlésienne Suite No. 1, "Carillon".....Georges Bizet

Section A

1. The chime ostinato rings out in French horns and strings.

2. The ostinato continues, along with the dance tune played by strings.

3. The music gets louder and louder. Section A ends with two chords, the first loud, the second, soft.

Section B

4. Two flutes play the quiet melody. Strings accompany.

5. Little by little the music gets louder. The chime ostinato returns at the end of Section B.

Section A

6. The dance tune returns. The chime ostinato continues. The piece ends with a ringing and clanging throughout the whole orchestra.

MEET THE COMPOSER

Georges Bizet   (1838–1875)

From early childhood, Georges Bizet showed a great interest in music; he learned the musical scale along with his alphabet. When he was nine years old, he entered the Paris Conservatory. He was an outstanding student and won many prizes for his piano playing and his compositions.

Throughout his life, Bizet was interested in writing music for the stage. Among his most famous works are the opera *Carmen* and two orchestral suites based on his incidental music to Daudet's play *L'Arlésienne*.

A FOUR-PHRASE SONG

Follow the phrase lines above the music as you listen to the recording of "I'm Gonna Sing." What can you discover about the phrases in the song?

I'm Gonna Sing   CD 2-29

African American Spiritual

1. I'm gon - na sing when the spir - it says "Sing." ____

I'm gon - na sing when the spir - it says "Sing." ____

I'm gon - na sing when the spir - it says "Sing." ____

And o - bey the spir - it of the Lord. ____

2. I'm gonna shout when the spirit says "Shout," *(3 times)*
   And obey the spirit of the Lord.

3. I'm gonna pray when the spirit says "Pray," *(3 times)*
   And obey the spirit of the Lord.

4. I'm gonna sing when the spirit says "Sing," *(3 times)*
   And obey the spirit of the Lord.

Courtesy Anonymous Donor

Lift Every Voice

Lift every voice and sing
Till earth and heaven ring,
Ring with the harmonies of liberty;
Let our rejoicing rise
High as the list'ning skies,
Let it resound loud as the rolling sea.
Sing a song full of the faith that the dark
past has taught us.
Sing a song full of the hope that the present
has brought us.
Facing the rising sun of our new day begun,
Let us march on till victory is won.

James Weldon Johnson

My Right Is an Equality with Other Americans *Elizabeth Catlett*

Meet the Artist

Elizabeth Catlett was born and raised in
Washington, D.C. As a little girl she was always
drawing and painting and in a high-school art
class, she made her first piece of sculpture—an
elephant carved from a bar of soap! Today
Elizabeth Catlett is regarded as one of
America's greatest African American artists. Her
work is exhibited in galleries across the United
States. The print shown above is one of a
number of Catlett's prints that illustrate James
Weldon Johnson's *Lift Every Voice and Sing*, an
exceptional book that was published in 1993.

Elizabeth Catlett

The Shape of a Melody

A melody can have tones that move upward or downward by step, tones that leap, and tones that repeat. The way tones move gives a melody its **contour**, or shape. How do the tones move in each phrase of this song?

Feasting by the Ocean   CD 3-1

Words by L. Golden   Song from Hawaii

1. Sun is ris - ing o - ver the o - cean,
2. Hur - ry now, the sun is ris - ing high - er,
3. Rea - dy now, come gath - er round the ta - ble,

Breez - es set the palm trees in mo - tion,
Dig the pit and start the fi - re,
Eat the *poi,* as much as you are a - ble,

Time to rise and start the prep - a - ra - tions,
Fish - er, bring your catch for cook - ing,
Roast - ed pig is yours for the ask - ing,

For the day of feast - ing has be - gun.
Soon the time for feast - ing will be here.
Feast - ing by the o - cean time is here.

The music in this listening selection begins with the sound of ocean waves, which the composer recorded late one night in Kona, Hawaii. What other sounds did the composer add to create "Mysterious Island"?

"Mysterious Island" from
Planet Drum .... Mickey Hart

CD 3-2

Name the Tune Game

Here are the beginnings of some songs you may know. Can you name each song by looking at the contour of the first phrase?

Same contour different levels

Happy Days   CD 3-3, 4

Words and Music by Norman Gimbel and Charles Fox

Sun - day, Mon - day, Hap - py Days, —

Tues - day Wednes - day, Hap - py Days, —

Thurs - day, Fri - day, Hap - py Days, —

Sat - ur - day, — what a day — Rock-in' all week with you. —

Follow the contour of the melody in each phrase as you listen to "Happy Days." How many phrases are there? Are any phrases alike?

"Happy Days" is the theme song from a television series. Do you have a favorite television series? Does it have a theme song that introduces every program? Can you sing or hum the theme? Use these bells to help you compose a television theme of your own.

This day is ours, _____ won't you be mine, _

This day is ours, _____ oh please be mine. _

These hap - py days are yours and mine,

These hap - py days are yours and mine, hap - py days.

SEQUENCES

Follow the contour of the melody as you listen to the recording of this song from the West Indies. Pay particular attention to the short melody patterns in the color boxes. How are they alike? How are they different?

Wings of a Dove CD 3-5, 6

Folk Song from the West Indies

If I had the wings of a dove, If I had the wings of a dove,

I would fly, fly a - way,

fly _____ a - way _____ and be _____ at rest. *Fine*

Since I have no wings, Since I have no wings, Since I have no wings, how can I

fly? _____ Since I have no wings, Since I have no wings,

D.C. al Fine

Since I have no wings, I'm gon - na sing, sing, sing, sing.

Used by permission of Berandol Music Publishers. Markham, Ontario.

A variety of percussion instruments are found in the islands off the southeast coast of the United States. You will hear the warm sounds of a steel-drum band in this music from the West Indies.

El merecumbe
...........Steel Drum Band

CD 3-7

TEMPO & DYNAMICS

How do you think this song should be sung? Loud? Soft?
Slow? Fast? The words of the song might give you an idea.

Stars of the Heavens (*Las estrellitas del cielo*) CD 3-8

English Version by Aura Kontra   *Folk Song from Mexico*

Leisurely

Stars of the heav - ens are wink - ing,
Las es - tre - lli - tas del cie - lo

With sil - v'ry light they are twin - kling.
Bri - llan con su luz de pla - ta.

A heav - en - ly rid - er came jing - ling
Y San - tia - go las fué sem - bran - do

With sil - v'ry spurs, star - light sprin - kling.
Con sus es - pue - las de pla - ta.

Which of these parts will you choose to play in a performance of "Stars of the Heavens"?

On this recording you will hear a ballad from Israel sung by Joan Baez, a popular American folksinger. What can you say about her performance style?

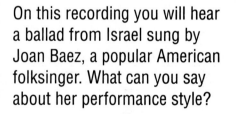

Dona, Dona ....
Sholom Secunda

CD 3-9

Music Creates a Mood

Felix Mendelssohn composed a group of pieces to accompany William Shakespeare's play *A Midsummer Night's Dream*. The piece Mendelssohn wrote to be performed between the first and second acts of the play is called "Scherzo." The piece played between the third and fourth acts is called "Nocturne."

As you listen to each piece, look at the words below. Which words suggest the **mood**, or feeling, of the music in each piece?

calm	quiet	excited	merry
gentle	peaceful	lively	cheerful

"Scherzo" and "Nocturne" from
A Midsummer Night's Dream..................Felix Mendelssohn
CD 3-10, 11

The first theme of each piece is notated below. When "Scherzo" and
"Nocturne" are played again, identify the instrument(s) that plays
each theme.

Theme from "Scherzo"

Theme from "Nocturne"

MEET THE COMPOSER

Felix Mendelssohn was born into a happy,
music-loving family in Germany in 1809.
Both he and his sister showed early signs
of great musical talent. Their mother gave
them their first music lessons; soon they
were ready for further study with the best
teachers that could be found. Felix made
wonderful progress and began to write
music when he was ten years old.

As Felix was growing up, there were many
musical parties in the Mendelssohn home,
where famous musicians and artists of the
day gathered for Sunday evening concerts.
The program often contained one or more
compositions by the young Mendelssohn.

Felix Mendelssohn   (1809-1847)

AB form

River CD 3-12

Words and Music by Bill Staines

A

1. I was born in the path of the win - ter wind,
2. I've been to the cit - y and back a - gain,
3. Some - day when the flow - ers are bloom - ing still,

And was raised where the moun - tains are old. _____
I've been moved by some things that I've learned. _____
Some - day when the grass is still green, _____

The spring - time _____ wa - ters came danc - ing down,
Met a lot of _____ good peo - ple and I've called them my friends,
My roll - ing _____ riv - er will round the bend

I re - mem - ber the tales they told. _____
Felt the change when the sea - sons turned. _____
And flow in - to the o - pen sea. _____

The whis - tling _____ ways of my young - er days
I've heard all the songs that the child - ren sing
So here's to the rain - bow that's fol - lowed me here,

Too quick-ly have fad-ed on by. _____
And list-ened to love's mel-o-dies, _____
And here's to the friends that I know, _____

But all of the mem-or-ies lin-ger still,
I've felt my own mus-ic with-in me rise
And here's to the song that's with-in me now;

Like the light in a fad-ing sky. _____
Like the wind in the au-tumn trees. _____
I will sing it where'-er I go. _____

B REFRAIN

Riv-er, take me a-long, In your sun-shine sing me your song.

Ev-er mov-ing and wind-ing and _ free,

You roll-ing old riv-er, you chang-ing old riv-er,

Let's you and me, riv-er, Run down to the sea. _____

Listen for AB form in this piece for guitar.

CD 3-13

Minuetto in D Major............Fernando Sor

Form 71

Don't Count Your Chickens

CD 3-14, 15

Words and Music by Carmino Ravosa

(A) G   G

Don't count your chick-ens be - fore they hatch, Be - fore they hatch,

G   G

be - fore they hatch. Don't count your chick-ens be - fore they hatch,

G   D₇   G

Be - fore they hatch, *(clap   clap)* they   hatch!

B   C

Don't you   plan a-bout to-mor-row, 'cause to - mor-row does-n't come un - til to -

© 1971 Carmino Ravosa

This song has two different sections—A and B. Listen to the music to find out what happens at the end of each section.

You will hear two pieces. One is very old—from the sixteenth century. The other was written 400 years later, in the twentieth century. Can you discover what these pieces have in common?

CD 3-16

"Bergerette" from *Suite* .... Anonymous

CD 3-17

"Galop" from *Suite No. 2* .... Igor Stravinsky

mor - row; Have a lot - ta fun to - day be-cause to - mor-row may just bring a lot-ta sor - row. Don't you sor - row.

Don't count your chick-ens be - fore they hatch, Be - fore they hatch, be - fore they hatch. Don't count your chick-ens be - fore they hatch, Be - fore they hatch, (clap clap) they hatch!

ABA FORM

Show that you hear the two sections in this song by doing a different hand pattern for each section.

Fisk Singers

Great Day   CD 3-18

African American Spiritual

A **D**

Great ___ day! Great day, the right-eous march-in',

Great ___ day! God's gon-na build up Zi-on's walls.   **A₇** **D** *Fine*

B

1. The char - iot rode on the moun - tain top, ___
2. This is the day of ___ ju - bi - lee, ___
3. We want no cow - ards ___ in our band, ___

God's gon - na build up Zi - on's walls,

My God he spoke and the char - iot stopped, __
The Lord he has set his __ peo - ple free, __
We call for val - iant __ heart - ed men, __

A₇   D   *D.C. al Fine*

God's gon - na build up Zi - on's walls.

MUSIC MAKERS

Do you find this pattern in section A or in section B of "Music, Music, Music"? Play the pattern on the bells every time it comes in the song. How many times will you play it?

Like all rock songs you might hear today, this popular song of the 1950s has a strong, steady beat. As you listen to *At the Hop*, clap the beat during section A and snap the beat during section B.

At the Hop ....Singer, Medora, and White

CD 3-22

Music, Music, Music CD 3-19, 20

Words and Music by Stephan Weiss and Bernie Baum

Ⓐ C

Put an-oth-er nick-el in, __ in the nick-el - o-de-on, __

G7 · · · · · · · C

All I want is lov-ing you __ and mu-sic, mu-sic, mu-sic!

I'd do an-y-thing for you. __ An-y-thing you'd want me to, __

G7

All I want is lov-ing you, __ and mu-sic, mu-sic, mu-sic!

Ⓑ G7 · · · · · · · · C

Clos - er, __ my dear, come clos - er, __ The ni-cest

G7 · · · · · · · · C · · · G7

part of an-y mel-o-dy __ is when you're sing-ing here with me. __

Ⓐ

So put an-oth-er nick-el in, __ in the nick-el - o-de-on, __

G7 · · · · · · · C

All I want is lov-ing you __ and mu-sic, mu-sic, mu-sic.

Three Different Sections

Think of three different hand motions. Then, as you listen to "Dry Bones," perform a different motion for each section of the song.

Dry Bones   CD 3-23, 24

African American Spiritual

A

E - ze-kiel cried, "Them dry — bones!" E - ze-kiel cried, "Them dry — bones!"

E - ze-kiel cried, "Them dry — bones!" Now hear the word of the Lord.

B

The foot bone con-nect - ed to the leg —— bone,

The leg bone con-nect - ed to the knee — bone,

The knee bone con-nect - ed to the thigh — bone,

The thigh bone con-nect - ed to the hip —— bone,

The hip bone con-nect-ed to the back bone,

The back bone con-nect-ed to the shoul - der bone,

The shoul - der bone con-nect - ed to the neck bone,

The neck bone con-nect - ed to the jaw bone,

The jaw bone con-nect - ed to the head bone, Now

hear the word of the Lord.

Them bones, them bones gon - na
Them bones, them bones, them

walk a - round, Them bones, them bones gon - na
dry bones, Them bones, them bones, them

walk a-round, Them bones, them bones gon - na walk a-round
dry bones, Them bones, them bones, them dry bones.

Now hear the word of the Lord.
Now hear the word of the Lord.

RONDO FORM

A B A C A

When you sang "Dry Bones," you sang a song that has three different sections. Now listen for the three different sections in a piece for electronic synthesizer. Following the call chart will help you hear how the three sections are used in a form called *rondo*.

Electronic Rondo .... Gershon Kingsley

CD 4-2

CALL CHART

1	A	
2	B	
3	A	
4	C	
5	A	

"School Rules Chant" Rondo

Believing in yourself and others is a good way to live your life at school and everywhere.

Use this chant for section A.

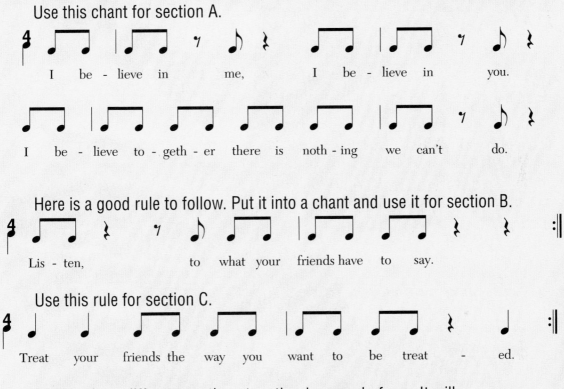

I be - lieve in me, I be - lieve in you.

I be - lieve to - geth - er there is noth - ing we can't do.

Here is a good rule to follow. Put it into a chant and use it for section B.

Lis - ten, to what your friends have to say.

Use this rule for section C.

Treat your friends the way you want to be treat - ed.

Put the three different sections together in a rondo form. It will look like this.

Listen for the rondo form in this piece. Do you know the name of the instrument that is playing?

Gigue en rondeau ....Jean-Philippe Rameau

CD 4-1

Let's DANCE!

On this recording, Misha Millington—the young girl in the yellow shirt—talks with Lisa Lequillou, the dance captain of the Broadway musical Tommy.

CD 4-3
Careers in Music—Lisa Lequillou

You will hear a piece by Mozart that is in rondo form. As you listen to the recording, think about how you might show the form through dance.

CD 4-4
"Romance" from A Little Night Music
.....................Wolfgang Amadeus Mozart

The world is full of sounds—long sounds, short sounds. Listen to the sounds around you right now. What do you hear?

Experiment making long and short sounds on classroom instruments. On which instruments can you make only short sounds? On which instruments can you make both long and short sounds?

Clap this short-short-long pattern as you listen to the recording of "Side by Side."

Side   by   side,   Side   by   side

Side by Side CD 4-5

Words and Music by Harry Woods

Oh! We ain't got a bar-rel of mon - ey,
Don't know what's com' - n' to - mor - row,

May - be we're rag - ged and fun - ny,
May - be it's trou - ble and sor - row,

But we'll trav - el a - long,_ sing-in' a song,_ side by side.
But we'll trav - el the road,_ shar-in' our load,_ side by side.

Through all kinds of weath - er, what if the sky should fall?____

Just as long as we're to - geth-er, it does-n't mat-ter at all;_____

When they've all had their quar - rels and part - ed,

We'll be the same as we start - ed,

Just trav - 'lin' a - long,_ sing-in' a song,_ side by side. ___

PATTERNS

Listen for the pattern of long and short sounds made by the English words of "At the Spring." On which words do you hear the longest sound?

At the Spring *(Koni au i ka wai)* CD 4-6

Words and Music by King Kalakaua   English Words by Liliana Wahine   Song from Hawaii

F

Of the cool wa - ters fresh at the spring,
Ko - ni au ko - ni au i ka wai,
koh - nee ahoo koh - nee ahoo ee kah wahee

C₇

Of their cool won - der now let us sing;
Ko - ni au i ka wai hu - i hui;
koh - nee ahoo ee kah wahee hoo - ee hoo ee

F   **B♭**

Of the gift of health that they give to all,
I - ka wai a - lii a - ke ki - ni la,
ee - kah wahee ah - lee ee ah - kay kee - nee lah

C₇   **F**

And the pleas - ure to us the wa - ters bring.
O - lu ai ka - no - ho - na o - ka lai.
oh - loo ahee kah - noh - hoh - nah oh kah lahee

Rhythm of the Words

Long and short sounds can be combined to make a rhythm pattern. Follow the rhythm pattern of each line of the song as you listen to the music.

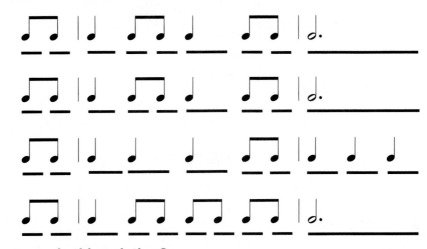

Can you find patterns in this painting?

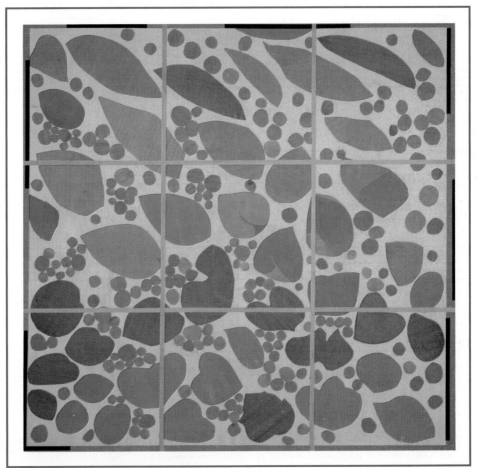

Ivy in Flower *Henri Matisse*

Rain Chant

Native American children take part in the songs and dances of their tribe. At an early age they learn how to beat the drum and shake rattles.

Breezes Are Blowing

Luiseno Indian Rain Chant   CD 4-7

Breez - es   are   blow - ing,   Blow - ing clouds of   wa - ter;

Breez - es   are   blow - ing,   Blow - ing clouds of   wa - ter;

On   my   face,   rain - ing,   Rain - ing from the   o - cean;

Breez - es   are   blow - ing,   Blow - ing clouds of   wa - ter.

Listen for rattles and drums in this
Native American music.

Zuni Rain Dance
.....................Traditional Native
American

CD 4-8

Near the end of this composition, you will
hear a melody that is a Zuni tune from
New Mexico.

Cloud Chamber Music
...................Harry Partch

CD 4-9

I Am Crying from Thirst

I am crying from thirst.
I am singing for rain.
The sky begins to weep,
for it sees me
singing and dancing
on the dry, cracked
earth.

Alonzo Lopez-Papago

INUIT SONG

When hunters return from a successful trip, they celebrate with their families. They accompany their songs by clapping hands and beating a drum or the cover of a large pan.

CD 4-10

The Returning Hunter

English Words by Elizabeth Whaley   Inuit Song

1. Sing the song of A - jung, Brave hunt - er A - jung,
2. Sing the song of Ka - lish, Keen fish - er Ka - lish,
3. Sing the song of Tee - ka, Bead - stitch-ing Tee - ka,

Brave hunt - er, bold and strong. Hunts for po - lar bear at night,
Keen fish - er, quick and true. In his kay - ak small and frail,
Bead - stitch-ing red on white, Sews a par - ka gay and bright,

Sends his spear in speed - y flight,
Braves the sea and wind and hail,
Mak - ing par - ka warm and light.

Hunt - ing car - i - bou, he shows no fright,
Spear - ing fish and e - ven gi - ant whale,
Sew - ing beads of red on hide of white,

O A - jung, Yai!
O Ka - lish, Yai!
O Tee - ka, Yai!

The Inuit's most important musical instrument is a large, shallow tambourine drum covered with caribou skin.

Other instruments such as rattles, flutes, and whistles are sometimes found, but by far the most important form of music is the song accompanied by the drum.

Listen to this Inuit song about a musk ox hunt.

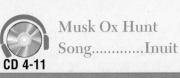

Musk Ox Hunt
Song.............Inuit

CD 4-11

A Ballad From Down Under

In Australia, men going from one job to another carry all their possessions in a blanket roll—a matilda.

Waltzing Matilda CD 4-12

Words by A. B. Patterson   Music by Maria Cowan

1. Once a jol-ly swag-man sat be-side the bil-la-bong,
2. Down came a jum-buck to drink be-side the bil-la-bong,

Un-der the shade of a coo-li-bah tree, And he
Up jumped the swag-man and seized him with glee, And he

sang as he sat and wait-ed by the bil-la-bong,
sang as he talked to that jum-buck in his tuck-er-bag,

"You'll come a-waltz-ing, Ma-til-da, with me."
"You'll come a-waltz-ing, Ma-til-da, with me."

REFRAIN

Waltz - ing Ma - til - da, waltz - ing Ma - til - da,
Waltz - ing Ma - til - da, waltz - ing Ma - til - da,

You'll come a-waltz - ing, Ma - til - da, with me. And he
You'll come a-waltz - ing, Ma - til - da, with me. And he

sang as he sat and wait - ed till his bil - ly boiled,
sang as he talked to that jum - buck in his tuck - er-bag,

"You'll come a-waltz - ing, Ma - til - da, with me."
"You'll come a-waltz - ing, Ma - til - da, with me."

3. Down came the stockman, riding on his thoroughbred,
Down came the troopers, one, two, three.
"Where's the jolly jumbuck you've got in your tuckerbag?
You'll come a-waltzing, Matilda, with me." *Refrain*

4. Up jumped the swagman and plunged into the billabong,
"You'll never catch me alive," cried he.
And his ghost may be heard as you ride beside the billabong,
"You'll come a-waltzing, Matilda, with me." *Refrain*

Listen for this pattern in a piece from a country far
from Australia.

La bamba ....Folk Song from Mexico

CD 4-13

Theme and Variations

On page 56 in your music book, you learned that the French composer Bizet wrote a group of pieces to accompany a play called L'Arlésienne—"The Woman of Arles." In an introduction, or overture, to the play, Bizet used a march tune based on an old French song as the theme of the piece.

Follow the chart as you listen to the music. It will help you hear how Bizet varied, or changed, the theme.

1. Theme: Strings play together.

2. Variation 1: Soft woodwinds play.

3. Variation 2: Gets louder and softer.

4. Variation 3: Slower; theme smooth; accompaniment has short tones.

5. Variation 4: Like a march; drums play.

6. Coda (ending section): Loud, soft, ends softly.

Try creating your own variations on this familiar tune.

Bizet: *L'Arlésienne Suite No. 1*, Overture
CD 4-16

YOUR VOICE IS YOU

Your voice has a special sound (**tone color**) whether you use it to whisper, speak, shout, or sing. Every person in the world has a voice that sounds different from any other voice.

Listen for the tone color of the voices that sing on the recording of "The Foolish Frog." Can you tell who is singing?

The Foolish Frog   CD 4-17

Words and Music by Charles L. Seeger and Pete Seeger

Way down yon - der in the Yank - et - y Yank, ___

A bull - frog jumped from bank to bank,

Just be - cause he'd noth - ing bet - ter for to do. ___

He stubbed his toe and fell in the wa - ter,

You could hear him hol - ler for a mile and a quar - ter

On this recording, Pete Seeger uses his voice in a variety of ways as he tells the story of the foolish frog.

CD 4-18

The Story of the Foolish Frog......................Pete Seeger

C₇ ... F

Just be-cause he'd noth-ing bet-ter for to do. _____

F ... D₇ ... Gm

There are lots of folks just like that fool-ish frog of mine, _

C₇ ... F

frog of mine, _ get them-selves in trou-ble just to pass the time, _

D₇ ... Gm

pass the time. _ Yes, lots of folks just like that fool-ish frog of mine, _

C₇ ... F

frog of mine, _ just be-cause they've noth-ing bet-ter for to do.

Candle on the Water

Words and Music by Al Kasha and Joel Hirschhorn

What kind of singing voice do you hear on the recording of "Candle on the Water"?

Cir-cling in the air, light-ed by a prayer.

I'll be your can-dle on the wa-ter,

This flame in-side of me will grow.

Keep hold-ing on, you'll make it, Here's my hand so take it,

Look for me reach-ing out to show as sure as riv-ers

flow, I'll nev-er let you go, I'll nev-er let you go,

I'll nev-er let you go. ___

A CABALLERO'S SONG

The caballero in this song serenades his sweetheart as he stands in the garden beneath her window.

Cielito lindo

CD 4-21,22

English Words by Alice Firgau   Folk Song from Mexico

1. De la sie - rra mo - re - na. Cie - li - to
1. *From the dark,___ dis - tant moun-tain, Cie - li - to*

lin - do, Vie - nen ba - jan - do,_____
lin - do, I_____ see de - scend - ing._____

Un par de o - ji - tos ne - gros, Cie - li - to
Your dark eyes___ flash - ing bright - ly, Cie - li - to

lin - do, de_____ con - tra - ban - do._____
lin - do, love's___ mes - sage send - ing._____

REFRAIN

Ay, ay, ay, ay!_____ Can - ta y no
Ay, ay, ay, ay!_____ Sing, sing with

In this listening selection, you will hear another version of *Cielito lindo*. How is this performance different from the performance you heard on the song recording?

llo - res. _____ Por - que can - tan - do se_a - le - gran, Cie -
glad - ness. _____ For in those hearts that are sing - ing, Cie -

1.,2   **Repeat REFRAIN last time only**

- li - to lin - do, los co - ra - zo - nes. _____
- li - to lin - do, there is no sad - ness. _____

Last time only on repeat of the REFRAIN

lin - do, los co - ra - zo - nes. _____
lin - do, there is no sad - ness. _____

2. Ese lunar que tienes, Cielito lindo,
   Junto a la boca,
   No se lo des a nadie, Cielito lindo,
   que a mi me toca. *Refrain*

2. *For your kisses, my lovely Cielito lindo,*
   My heart is aching,
   And when I can't be near you, Cielito lindo,
   my heart is breaking. Refrain

Cielito lindo
................Folk Song from Mexico
CD 4-23

Solo and Chorus

Follow the music as you listen to the recording. Join in on the chorus parts when you can.

Limbo Like Me CD 4-24

Words and Music Adapted by Massie Patterson and Sammy Heyward

Solo C ... F C *Chorus* G7 C
I want a girl to lim-bo like me; Lim-bo, lim-bo like me.

Solo C ... F C *Chorus* C G7 C
Lim-bo, lim-bo, lim-bo like me; Lim-bo, Lim-bo like me.

Solo C ... F C *Chorus* C G7 C
Ev-'ry bod-y lim-bo like me; Lim-bo, lim-bo like me.

Solo C ... F C *Chorus* C G7 C
My lit-tle goat can lim-bo like me; Lim-bo, lim-bo like me.

Solo C ... F C *Chorus* G7 C
Mon-key try to lim-bo like me; Lim-bo, lim-bo like me.

Listen for the solo-chorus parts in this selection.

El tilingo lingo
..................Folk Song from Mexico

CD 4-25

Vocal Combinations

You can hear solo voices in the recording of the song on page 98. "Candle on the Water" is sung by a woman.
Voices can also sing together in many different combinations.

Listen for the voices in this recording of "America, the Beautiful." How many voices do you hear?

America, the Beautiful, Version 1.....Bates/Ward
CD 4-26

Here is another version of "America, the Beautiful." Who is singing in this version?

America, the Beautiful, Version 2.....Bates/Ward
CD 4-27

On this recording you will hear another combination of voices. Do you hear many voices or few voices in this version of the song?

America, the Beautiful, Version 3.....Bates/Ward
CD 4-28

Can you finish these sentences?

A combination of two voices singing in parts is called a

_____

A combination of three voices singing in parts is called a

_____

A combination of many voices singing in parts is called a

_____

Duet

Trio

Chorus

A SPECIAL VOCAL ARRANGEMENT

The woman at the piano in the photograph below is Linda Twine—composer, conductor, arranger, music director, church musician. She made a special vocal arrangement of "Walk in Jerusalem" just for you. On the recording *Careers in Music,* Ms. Twine is interviewed by her good friend and student Jeanine Levenson.

 Careers in Music—Linda Twine

CD 5-3

Walk in Jerusalem CD 5-1, 2

African American Spiritual

A REFRAIN

I want _____ to be read - y,

I want _____ to be read - y, _____

I want _____ to be read - y

Fine

to walk in Je - ru - sa - lem just like John.

B VERSE

1. John said the cit - y was just four square, _
2. John, oh, ___ John, _ what do you say? ___

Walk in Je - ru - sa - lem just like John,
Walk in Je - ru - sa - lem just like John,

And he de - clared he'd meet me there! _
That I'll be there in the com - ing day, ___

D.C. al Fine

Walk in Je - ru - sa - lem just like John.
Walk in Je - ru - sa - lem just like John.

GOSPEL, A Special Style

Gospel singing started in black Baptist churches in the 1920s. Two kinds of gospel singing became popular. One was an all-male quartet. The other was a chorus with soloists. Both styles have slow songs as well as fast rocking ones. Both types of gospel singing influenced rock and roll, especially gospel's use of call and response and strong rhythms. The man considered to be the father of gospel music is Thomas A. Dorsey. Dorsey composed more than 400 gospel songs.

Staple Singers

Meet the Father of Gospel Music

Thomas A. Dorsey   (1899-1993)

Thomas A. Dorsey was born near Atlanta, Georgia, in 1899. Although there was no piano at home, Dorsey was determined to learn to play. Four days a week he walked four miles each way to a teacher. Within two years he played well enough to earn money playing for local Saturday night dances. Dorsey became an accomplished blues and jazz pianist and eventually studied music at the Chicago College of Composition and Arranging.

In 1921, Dorsey joined the Pilgrim Baptist Church in Chicago. He decided he wanted to compose gospel music and gave up playing blues. His music was a new style of gospel influenced by the blues. It was emotional music with rocking rhythms.

Dorsey's songs are known all over the world and have been translated into many different languages. Many people today are glad that Thomas A. Dorsey gave up playing the blues and put his talent and energy into gospel music. These are the many people who have felt the joy and happiness of gospel music.

Listen to three different performances of gospel singing.

Anyhow ....R. Staples
CD 5-4

Said I Wasn't Gonna Tell Nobody ....Bradford
CD 5-4

Don't Knock ....R. Staples
CD 5-4

Pop Song and Partners

You will hear a recording of the three short songs that are printed on this page and the next page. Follow the melody of each song as you listen.

One Bottle of Pop CD 5-6, 7

Traditional

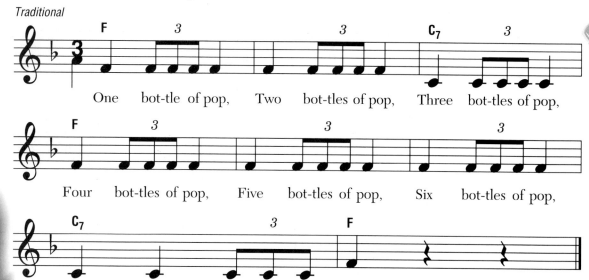

One bot-tle of pop, Two bot-tles of pop, Three bot-tles of pop,

Four bot-tles of pop, Five bot-tles of pop, Six bot-tles of pop,

Sev'n, sev'n bot - tles of Pop!

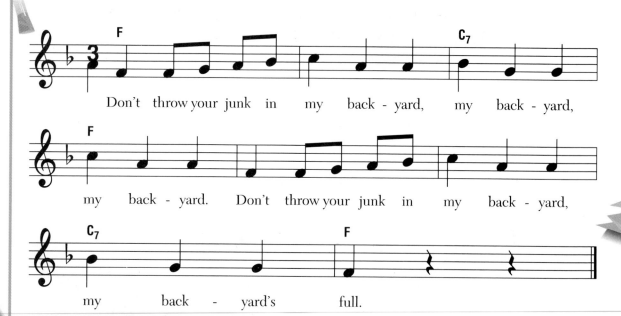

Don't throw your junk in my back - yard, my back - yard,

my back - yard. Don't throw your junk in my back - yard,

my back - yard's full.

When you and your classmates can sing each short song, you will be ready to create harmony by singing all three songs at the same time.

Autoharp Strums

Here are three autoharp parts you can use to accompany "One Bottle of Pop." Will you use the same strum for each short melody or will you choose a different strum for each song?

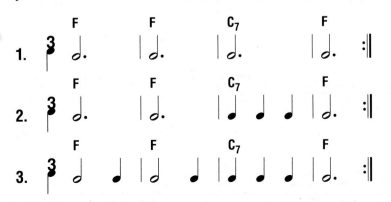

A TWO-PART ROUND

Tap or snap the steady beat as you listen to the recording of this humorous song about a frog.

Frog Music CD 5-8

Folk Song from Canada

There once was a frog who jumped in a bog And played the bass fid-dle In the mid-dle of a pud-dle, What a mud-dle! "Bet-ter go 'round! Bet-ter go 'round!" _____ His mu-sic was short, For soon he was caught, And now in the mid-dle of a grid-dle he is fry-ing and is cry-ing: "Rath-er be drown'd! Rath-er be drown'd!" _____

The frog in this poem is a good deal
smarter than the frog in the song!

Grandfather Frog

Fat green frog sits by the pond,
Big frog, bull frog, grandfather
frog.
Croak—croak—croak.
Shuts his eye, opens his eye,
Rolls his eye, winks his eye,
Waiting for
A little fat fly.
Croak, croak.
I go walking down by the pond,
I want to see the big green frog,
I want to stare right into his eye,
Rolling, winking, funny old eye,
But oh! he hears me coming by,
Croak—croak—
SPLASH!

Louise Seaman Bechtel

A 4-PART ROUND

The kookaburra is a bird found in Australia. Its call sounds like loud laughter.

In order to sing "Kookaburra" as a four-part round, you must be able to do two things well.

Sing the melody without the recording.

Keep the beat steady.

Kookaburra   CD 5-9

Words and Music by Marion Sinclair

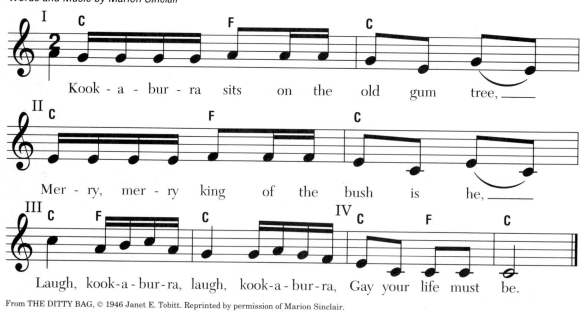

I C   F   C
Kook - a - bur - ra sits on the old gum tree, ____

II C   F   C
Mer - ry, mer - ry king of the bush is he, ____

III C F C   IV C F C
Laugh, kook-a - bur - ra, laugh, kook-a - bur - ra, Gay your life must be.

From THE DITTY BAG, © 1946 Janet E. Tobitt. Reprinted by permission of Marion Sinclair.

Organize an orchestra for "Kookaburra." Will you play a rhythm pattern on a percussion instrument, a melody pattern on the bells, or will you strum an accompaniment on the autoharp?

Percussion Patterns

Can you find these patterns in the song?

Bell Patterns

Which ostinato pattern will you play in the "Kookaburra" orchestra?

Autoharp Pattern

Follow the chord names in the music as you strum this steady-beat pattern.

Countermelodies

There are two different melodies in this song. Each one has a personality of its own. The two melodies can also be sung together to create harmony.

The Inchworm
from *Hans Christian Andersen*   CD 5-10

Words and Music by Frank Loesser

Melody 1

Inch-worm, inch-worm, meas-ur-ing the mar-i-golds.

You and your a-rith-me-tic, you'll prob-a-bly go far. _____

Inch-worm, inch-worm, meas-ur-ing the mar-i-golds.

Seems to me you'd stop and see how beau-ti-ful they are. _____

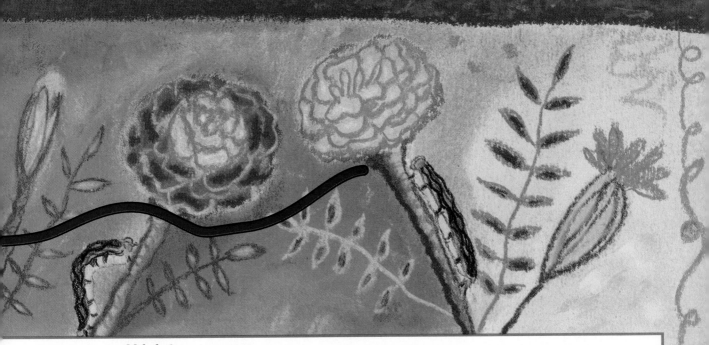

Melody 2

Two and two are four, four and four are eight,

Eight and eight are six - teen, six - teen and six -

teen are thir - ty - two. Two and two are four,

four and four are eight. Eight and eight

are six - teen, six - teen and six - teen are thir - ty - two.

An American Work Song

Many Irish immigrants found work laying the tracks of the first transcontinental railroad. The Irish wit and love of singing helped the workers survive the hardships of their job.

As you listen to this Irish American railroad song, tap or clap the steady beat. It will help you feel the rhythm that made the work a little easier.

Paddy Works on the Railway CD 5-11

Irish American Railroad Song

1. In eight-een hun-dred and for-ty-one I put my cor-du-roy breech-es on, I put my cor-du-roy breech-es on to work up-on the rail-way.

Add a Countermelody

Here is a countermelody to sing with the refrain of the song.

Countermelody (Refrain)

Fil - li - mee - oo - ree-oo-ree-ay, Fil - li - mee - oo - ree-oo-ree-ay,

Fil - li - mee - oo - ree - oo - ree - ay, Oo - ree - ay. ____

REFRAIN

Gm   Bb

Fil - li - mee-oo - ree - oo - ree - ay,   Fil - li - mee-oo - ree - oo - ree-ay,

Gm   D7   Gm

Fil - li-mee-oo - ree - oo - ree-ay,   To work up-on the rail - way.

2. In eighteen hundred and forty-two
    I left the old world for the new,
    Oh, spare me the luck that brought me through
    To work upon the railway. *Refrain*

3. It's "Pat, do this," and "Pat, do that,"
    Without a stocking or cravat,
    And nothing but an old straw hat,
    While working on the railway. *Refrain*

THE MARCH KING

Three Themes

On this recording you will hear three themes from Sousa's best-known march.

CD 5-12

The Stars and Stripes Forever Themes
................John Philip Sousa

Theme 1

Theme 2

Theme 3

Listen for the three themes on this recording of Sousa's best-known march.

CD 5-13 *The Stars and Stripes Forever* ....
John Philip Sousa

Sousa wrote words for this march. When you have heard the piece several times, try singing them to the melody of Theme 3 when it comes in the music.

Hurrah for the flag of the free,
May it wave as our standard forever,
The gem of the land and the sea,
The banner of all the right!
Let despots remember the day
When our fathers with mighty endeavor
Proclaimed as they marched in the fray
That by their might and by their right
It waves forever!

National Portrait Gallery, Smithsonian Institution/Art Resource, NY

John Philip Sousa *Harry Franklin Waltman*

MEET THE COMPOSER

John Philip Sousa   (1854–1932)

John Philip Sousa is known as the March King of the world. He was born and grew up in our nation's capital—Washington, D.C. Even as a little boy, he knew he wanted to be a musician. He often went to band rehearsals with his father, who played trombone in the United States Marine Band—the official band of the President of the United States. When Sousa was 26 years old, he became the director of this band and wrote some of his finest marches for it.

Sousa composed more than 100 marches during his lifetime. Many of these are played today by high school, college, and community bands throughout America. *The Stars and Stripes Forever* was Sousa's favorite march—it is known all over the world.

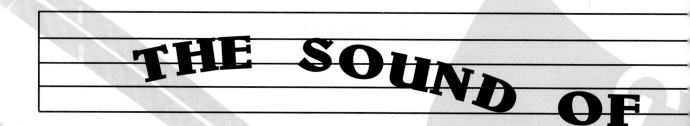

THE SOUND OF

An orchestra is made up of four families of instruments. Can you name an instrument from each of these families?

- Woodwinds
- Strings
- Brass
- Percussion

In the photograph below, find instruments that belong to each of the four families.

AN ORCHESTRA

One of the pieces you might hear at an orchestra concert is "Russian Sailor's Dance" by the composer Glière. He based the composition on this old Russian folk song.

Theme

Listen for all the families of instruments as they play together in this composition.

"Russian Sailor's Dance" from *The Red Poppy*
..................Reinhold Glière

CD 5-14

THE SOUND OF STRINGS

The violin, viola, cello, and string bass are members of the string family. Although their shapes are similar, their sizes vary from small to very large.

The string instruments are usually bowed. The sound is produced by drawing a bow across the strings. The pitch is low if the string is long and heavy, higher if the string is shorter and lighter.

Listen for the instruments of the string family in these pieces.

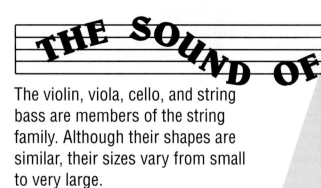

CD 5-15

We Gather Together for Strings

CD 5-16

Tales from the Latin Woods (strings) ....David Eddleman

THE SOUND OF WOODWINDS

The flute, oboe, clarinet, and bassoon are members of the woodwind family. All the instruments of this family were originally made of wood. Today the flute and sometimes the clarinet are made of metal or other material.

The woodwind instruments are played by blowing across or into the tube of the instrument. The air column inside the tube is set in vibration and tones are produced. Different pitches are created by changing the length of the column of air. The pitch is low if the column of air is long, high if the column of air is shorter.

Listen for the instruments of the woodwind family in these pieces.

We Gather Together for Woodwinds

CD 5-17

Tales from the Latin Woods (woodwinds)
...................David Eddleman

CD 5-18

The trumpet, trombone, French horn and tuba are members of the brass family. They are sometimes called brass wind instruments because the player blows into a mouthpiece to create the tone.

Each instrument consists of a long metal tube with a mouthpiece at one end and a bell-shaped opening at the other. The pitch is low if the tube is long. The pitch is high if the tube is short.

Listen for the instruments of the brass family in these pieces.

CD 5-19

We Gather Together for Brass

Tales from the Latin Woods (brass)
.................David Eddleman

CD 5-20

Percussion instruments are played by being struck or shaken. What classroom instruments pictured below are played by striking? By shaking? Experiment.

Each of the five percussion instruments used in this composition is played by striking.

Tales from the Latin Woods (Percussion)
....................David Eddleman

CD 5-21

THE SOUND OF PERCUSSION

The members of the percussion family come in many different shapes and sizes. They are all played by being struck with sticks, hammers, or hands, or by being shaken or scraped.

Listen for the instruments of the percussion family in this piece by a famous Mexican composer.

Toccata for Percussion ....Carlos Chávez

CD 5-22

MEET THE COMPOSER

Carlos Chávez   1899–1978

Carlos Chávez was born in Mexico City. He traced his paternal ancestry to the early Spanish settlers in Mexico. Chávez made many contributions to the cultural life of his country. For many years he was the director of the National Conservatory of Mexico. He organized and conducted one of the finest symphony orchestras Mexico ever had and appeared many times as a guest conductor in the United States.

Chávez had a deep interest in the people who lived in Mexico before the time of Cortes. He heard the music of Mexican Indians when he was a child. Later he became interested in the music of the Mayas, Aztecs, and Toltecs. He studied instruments that were preserved in museums and imagined the sounds those ancient instruments might make.

THE SOUND OF

Band music has always been popular in our country. In the early 1900s, going to the Sunday band concert in the park was a favorite pastime.

Today, in the fall, high school and college marching bands all over America perform during half time at football games. Band music may also be heard in concert halls.

A concert band is made up of wind instruments and percussion. Can you identify any of the instruments in the concert band shown in the photograph?

A CONCERT BAND

Theme 1

Theme 2

"Fantasia on Dargason" from *Suite for Band, No. 2*
....................Gustav Holst

CD 5-23

132

THEMES

Get ready for a great adventure in
the "Theme Connection."

There'll be music in the air no
matter where you go.

Through the music in this section of your book,
you'll travel across the country with the
forty-niners, ride with the cowhands on the trail
from Montana to Mexico, and take a trip
down the Grand Canyon with pony and pack burro.

You'll cross the ocean on a whaling ship
and visit Africa, Asia, and other faraway places.

There'll be music in the air as you
salute your country with poetry and song and
celebrate other special occasions with holiday
songs from near and far.

Are you ready for the great adventure?

section 2

Sounds of the Sea

With your finger, trace the contour of the melody as you listen to this folk song. How does the melody line help you imagine the great waves of the sea?

Windy Old Weather   CD 5-25

Folk Song from England

F .... C₇

1. As we were a - sail - ing off Haze - bor - ough light,

C₇ .... F

A - haul - ing and trawl - ing and pull - ing all night,

F .... B♭

It was win - dy old weath-er, boys, storm - y old weath-er,

C₇ .... F

When the wind blows, we'll all go to - geth - er.

2. Then up jumped the herring, the king of the sea.
   Says he to the skipper, "Look under your lea."
   For it's windy old weather, . . .

3. Then up jumped the mack'rel with stripes on his back.
   "Look out you old skipper, it's time to turn back."
   For it's windy old weather, . . .

The editors of Silver Burdett Ginn have made every attempt to verify the sources of "Windy Old Weather." We believe it to be in the public domain.

In a tribute to the earth, composer Paul Winter used the sound of a real whale in this unusual composition.

"Ocean Child" from *Earth: Voices of a Planet*
...................Paul Winter

CD 5-26

The Song of the Sea Wind   CD 5-27

How it sings, sings, sings,
    Blowing sharply from the sea-line,
With an edge of salt that stings;
    How it laughs aloud, and passes,
    As it cuts the close cliff-grasses;
        How it sings again, and whistles
        As it shakes the stout sea-thistles—
        How it sings!

How it shrieks, shrieks, shrieks,
    In the crannies of the headland,
In the gashes of the creeks;
    How it shrieks once more, and catches
    Up the yellow foam in patches:
        How it whirls it out and over
        To the corn-field and the clover—
        How it shrieks!

How it roars, roars, roars,
    In the iron under-caverns,
In the hollows of the shores;
    How it roars anew, and thunders,
    As the strong hull splits and sunders:
        And the spent ship, tempest driven,
        On the reef lies rent and riven—
        How it roars!

How it wails, wails, wails,
    In the tangle of the wreckage,
In the flapping of the sails;
    How it sobs away, subsiding,
    Like a tired child after chiding;
        And across the ground-swell rolling,
        You can hear the bell-buoy tolling—
        How it wails!

Austin Dobson

A Song of the Sea

In the old sailing-ship days, whaling crews signed on for voyages that sometimes lasted for three years. The work was hard and often dangerous. But in the evening, after the day's work was done, the whalers whiled away the time by singing. This is one of the songs they sang.

The Whale　CD 5-28

Old Whaling Song

1. 'Twas in eight - een hun - dred and fif - ty - three
And of June the thir - teenth __ day,
That our gal - lant ship her __ an - chor __ weighed,
And for Green - land bore __ a - way, brave boys,
And for Green - land bore __ a - way.

2. The lookout in the crosstrees stood,
   With his spyglass in his hand.
   "There's a whale, there's a whale, there's a whalefish," he cried,
   "And she blows at every span, brave boys,
   And she blows at every span."

3. The captain stood on the quarter-deck,
   And a fine little man was he.
   "Overhaul! Overhaul! Let your davit-tackles fall,
   And launch your boats for sea, brave boys,
   And launch your boats for sea."

4. Now the boats were launched and the men aboard,
   And the whale was in full view;
   Resolv-ed was each seaman bold
   To steer where the whalefish blew, brave boys,
   To steer where the whalefish blew.

5. We struck that whale, the line paid out,
   But she gave a flourish with her tail;
   The boat capsized and four men were drowned,
   And we never caught that whale, brave boys,
   And we never caught that whale.

You will hear a real humpback whale singing at the end of this music.

And God Created Great Whales
......................Alan Hovhaness
CD 6-1

Men worked to the rhythm of this old song as they laid the first railroad tracks in America.

I've Been Working on the Railroad CD 6-2

Work Song from the United States

1. I've been work-ing on the rail - road, All the live-long day;
I've been work-ing on the rail - road, Just to pass the time a - way.
Don't you hear the whis-tle blow - ing? Rise up so ear-ly in the morn.
Don't you hear the cap-tain shout - ing: "Di - nah, blow your horn!"

Percussion Parts

Play one of these parts to accompany the singing.

Team up with two friends and try playing all three patterns to accompany the song.

2. Dinah won't you blow, Dinah won't you blow,
   Dinah won't you blow your horn?
   Dinah won't you blow, Dinah won't you blow,
   Dinah, won't you blow your horn?

3. Someone's in the kitchen with Dinah,
   Someone's in the kitchen, I know.
   Someone's in the kitchen with Dinah,
   Strummin' on the old banjo.

4. Fee, Fie, Fiddle-ee I O,
   Fee, Fie, Fiddle-ee I O.
   Fee, Fie, Fiddle-ee I O,
   Strummin' on the old banjo.

ALL ABOARD

The title of this song tells you the name of one of the first railroads running west out of Chicago. How many times do you hear the name in the refrain of the song?

Rock Island Line   CD 6-3

Railroad Song   *New Words and New Arrangement by Huddie Ledbetter*
Edited with New Additional Material by Alan Lomax

REFRAIN
F
I say the Rock Is - land Line is a might-y good road, —

F   C₇
I say the Rock Is - land Line is the road to ride. —

F
I say the Rock Is - land Line is a might-y good road, —

F   B♭   F   B♭
If you want to ride it, got to ride it like you find it,

F   B♭   C₇   F   *Fine*
Get your tick-et at the sta-tion for the Rock Is - land line.

VERSE

1. May be right and I may be wrong, —

C₇ F *D.C. al Fine*

Know you're gon - na miss me ____ when I'm gone.

2. A, B, C, double X, Y, Z,
   Cats in the cupboard, but they don't see me. *Refrain*

Listen for train sounds in this humorous selection by The King's Singers.

The Railroad Cars Are Coming

The great Pacific railway
For California hail!
Bring on the locomotive,
Lay down the iron rail;
Across the rolling prairies,
Through mountain valleys grand,
The railroad cars are coming, humming,
Through the prairie land.
The prairie dogs in dog town,
The rattlesnake and quail
Will see the cars a-coming,
Just flying down the rail.
Amid the purple sagebrush,
The antelope will stand
While railroad cars are coming, humming
Through the prairie land.

Traditional

"I'm a Train" from *In Harmony*
.......................The King's Singers
CD 6-4

THE MUSIC OF A GREAT LOCOMOTIVE

Instruments of Power   *Thomas Hart Benton*

Equitable Trust Corp., New York

A Musical Journey

As you listen to the music of *Pacific 231*, follow the locomotive's progress from beginning to end.

CD 6-5

Pacific 231 ....Arthur Honegger

The following program notes may help you hear some of the things that are going on in the music.

- The great engine is at a standstill, gathering steam.
- The big wheels begin to turn slowly; the locomotive gets underway.
- The locomotive begins to move more quickly, gathering speed.
- The train rushes through the night.
- The great engine slows up.
- The big wheels finally grind to a stop.

Train Rhythms

Here are some rhythm patterns that the composer used in *Pacific 231*. The syllables and words under the notes may help you chant the patterns.

Sh,   sh,   sh,   sh

Click - clack,   click - clack,   click - clack,   click - clack

Ch,   ch,   ch,   ch - ch

Here comes the train,   Here comes the train.

MEET THE COMPOSER

Arthur Honegger   (1892–1953)

The composer Arthur Honegger was born in France. As a young man he was a fine athlete and was interested in all kinds of sports. Honegger also loved trains and thought of them as roaring giants of power and speed. It is not surprising that he decided to write a piece that would give the feeling of a locomotive. The locomotive that inspired him was an engine of the Pacific type, model number 231. It weighed 300 tons and was designed to pull heavy loads at great speed.

Honegger's composition *Pacific 231* was first performed in Paris, France, in 1923.

SONGS OF THE VENDORS

Here is a song that was sung by street sellers in ancient China. The people knew which seller was in the neighborhood because each one had a special song to sing. Who are the sellers in this song? What are they selling?

Feng Yang Song

Folk Song from China **CD 6-6**

1. Sing the Feng Yang Song; Sing it loud and long. Clash cym-bals,
2. Gifts for you have I, Kites that swoop and fly; Small trin-kets,

beat the drum, Strike the met-al gong! We are the ven-dors who
man-y toys, All of you may buy. Pa-per of gold shin-ing,

trav-el all day long, Call-ing our wares to the Feng Yang Song.
Bam-boo smooth and strong, Call-ing the clear, ring-ing toy-man's song.

REFRAIN

Feng yang, feng yang, beat the gong, — Strike the clap-pers well.

Clash cym-bals, byah yah yang, Clash cym-bals, byah yah yang! *Brr* dong!

Brr dong! *Brr* dong yah feng yang, feng yang, *Brr*, beat the drum!

3. Shave I have for you,
   Smooth–neat and true.
   Trimming and cutting hair,
   All of that I do.
   Keenness and skill
   To my instruments belong,
   Calling the clear, ringing
   Barber's song. *Refrain*

4. Fortune's magic spell
   I know very well;
   Dry sticks of ancient wood
   Always good foretell.
   Come, try your luck
   For the sticks are never wrong,
   Calling the clear, ringing
   Fortune teller's song. *Refrain*

Marketplaces

The calls and shouts of vendors make exciting street music in the marketplaces all over the world. Here are some calls that might be heard in a marketplace. Try chanting the calls or try playing the rhythms on a drum or a tambourine.

1. Buy my silk, fine silk; Buy my silk, fine silk.

2. Come and buy veg'-ta-bles! Come and buy veg'-ta-bles!

3. Gar-lic and car-a-way! Gar-lic and car-a-way!

4. Egg-plant! Fresh to-day! Egg-plant! Fresh to-day!

TORTILLAS FOR SALE

In this song, the street vendor calls his wares—crispy little pancakes called *tortillas*—as he passes by the doorstep of the girl he loves.

The Tortilla Vendor *(El tortillero)* **CD 6-7, 8**

English words by Alice Firgau *Folk Song from Chile*

1. Night has fal - len, deep the dark - ness,
1. *No - che_os - cu - ra na - da, ve - o,*

But my lan - tern light is bright;
pe - ro lle - vo mi fa - rol;

I am pass - ing by your door - step,
por tus puer - tas voy pa - san - do

Sing - ing love songs in the night. _____
y can - tan - do con a - mor._____

REFRAIN

But _____ while I'm sing - ing, _____ My _____
Mas, _____ voy can - tan - do _____ Con _____

_ heart is break - ing. _____ "Who'll buy _____ my
_ har - ta pe - na. _____ "¿Quién com - pra mis

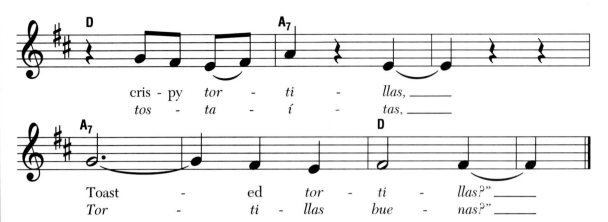

cris - py   tor - ti - llas, _____
tos - ta - í - tas, _____

Toast - ed   tor - ti - llas?" _____
Tor - ti - llas   bue - nas?" _____

2. Pretty lady, do have pity
   When you hear my vendor's cry,
   I am selling my tortillas
   Yet from you there's no reply,
   Refrain

3. With my basket and my lantern,
   Now it's time for me to go,
   This poor seller of tortillas
   Your sweet love will never know,
   Refrain

2. *Bella ingrata, no respondes*
   A mi grito placentero
   Cuando pasa por tu casa,
   Pregonando el tortillero.
   Refrain

3. *Ya me voy a retirar*
   Con mi canasto y farol,
   Sin tener tu compasión
   De este pobre tortillero.
   Refrain

Cowpunchers like to talk about the days of the Old West. After a hard day's work, they gather around the campfire to sing and to tell tall tales. Here is one of the tall tales they like the best.

Great Granddad CD 6-9

Cowboy Song from the United States

1. Great Grand-dad, when the land was young,
Barred the door with a wag-on tongue,
For the times was rough and the dan-gers great,
And he said his prayers both ear-ly and late.

2. He was a citizen tough and grim,
Danger was duck soup to him,
He ate corn pone and bacon fat,
Said his great grandson would starve on that.

3. Twenty-one children came to bless
The old man's house in the wilderness,
They slept on the floor with the dogs and cats,
And they hunted in the woods in their coonskin hats.

From THE COWBOY SINGS edited by Kenneth S. Clark. Copyright 1932 (renewed) Shawnee Press Inc. International copyright secured. All rights reserved. Used by permission.

Noonday Sun

Oh, I've ridden plenty of horses
    And I've broken a score in my time,
But there never was one
    Like the colt Noonday Sun—
Now there was a horse that was prime!
    Oh, yippi ippi ai—Oh, yippi ippi ay,
Now there was a horse that was prime!

She'd run up the side of a mountain
    Or she'd tackle a wildcat alone.
Oh, she stood twelve hands high
    And her proud shining eye
Would soften the heart of a stone.
    Oh, yippi ippi ai—Oh, yippi ippi ay,
Would soften the heart of a stone.

She'd splash through a treach'rous river,
    Or she'd tease for an apple or sweet,
She'd buck and she'd prance
    Or she'd do a square dance
On her four little white little feet.
    Oh, yippi ippi ai—Oh, yippi ippi ay,
On her four little white little feet.

But one night the rustlers stole her,
    They stole her and took her away.
Now the sun never shines,
    And the wind in the pines
Says, "You've lost your colt, lack-a-day!"
    Oh, yippi ippi ai—Oh, yippi ippi ay,
Says, "You've lost your colt, lack-a-day!"

Oh, I still have her bridle and saddle,
    And I still have her bare empty stall.
But there'll never be one
    Like the colt Noonday Sun,
And she'll never more come to my call!
    Oh, yippi ippi ai—Oh, yippi ippi ay,
And she'll never more come to my call!

Kathryn and Byron Jackson

Wells, Fargo and Company

The Wells Fargo Wagon

CD 6-13, 14

Words and Music by Meredith Willson

1. O - ho, the Wells Far-go Wag-on is a - com - in' down the street, oh
2. O - ho, the Wells Far-go Wag-on is a - com - in' down the street, oh

please let it be for me. ___ O - ho, the Wells Far-go Wag-on is a -
don't let him pass my door! ___ O - ho, the Wells Far-go Wag-on is a -

com-in' down the street, I wish, I wish I knew what it could be. _ I got a
com-in' down the street, I wish I knew what he was com-in' for. _ I got some

box of ma-ple su-gar on my birth-day. _ In March I got a gray mack-i -
sal-mon from Se-at-tle last Sep-tem-ber. _ And I ex-pect a new rock-in'

naw. And once I got some grape-fruit from Tam-pa. Mont-gom-'ry
chair. I hope I get my rai - sins from Fres-no. The D. A.

Here is a song from *The Music Man*, a musical comedy about a salesman who comes to River City, Iowa, to organize a town band. You will find another song from *The Music Man* on page 50 in your book.

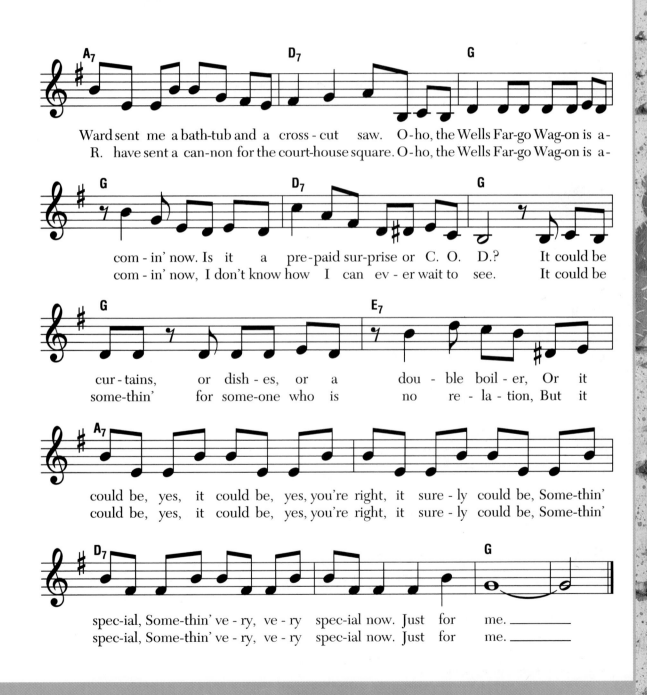

Ward sent me a bath-tub and a cross-cut saw. O-ho, the Wells Far-go Wag-on is a-
R. have sent a can-non for the court-house square. O-ho, the Wells Far-go Wag-on is a-

com-in' now. Is it a pre-paid sur-prise or C. O. D.? It could be
com-in' now, I don't know how I can ev-er wait to see. It could be

cur-tains, or dish-es, or a dou-ble boil-er, Or it
some-thin' for some-one who is no re-la-tion, But it

could be, yes, it could be, yes, you're right, it sure-ly could be, Some-thin'
could be, yes, it could be, yes, you're right, it sure-ly could be, Some-thin'

spec-ial, Some-thin' ve-ry, ve-ry spec-ial now. Just for me. _____
spec-ial, Some-thin' ve-ry, ve-ry spec-ial now. Just for me. _____

BALLAD OF A GIANT FREIGHTER

Follow the story of the *Edmund Fitzgerald* as you listen to the recording.

The Wreck of the "Edmund Fitzgerald"

CD 6-15

Words and Music by Gordon Lightfoot

1. The leg-end lives on from the Chip-pe-wa on down
   With a load of iron ore twenty-six thou-sand tons more

of the big lake they called "Git-chee Gu-mee,"
than the *Ed-mund Fitz-ger-ald* weighed emp-ty,

The lake, it is said, nev-er ___ gives up her dead
that good ship and true was a ___ bone to be chewed

when the skies of No-vem-ber turn gloom-y. _____
when the "Gales of No-vem-ber" came ear-ly. _____

© 1976 Moose Music Inc.

2. The ship was the pride of the American side
coming back from some mill in Wisconsin.
As the big freighters go it was bigger than most
with a crew and good captain well seasoned,
concluding some terms with a couple of steel
    firms when they left fully loaded for Cleveland.
And later that night when the ship's bell rang,
could it be the north wind they'd been feelin'?

3. The wind in the wires made a tattletale sound
and a wave broke over the railing.
And ev'ry man knew as the captain did too
'twas the witch of November come stealin',
The dawn came late and the breakfast had to wait
when the gales of November came slashin'.
When afternoon came it was freezin' rain
in the face of a hurricane west wind.

4. When suppertime came the old cook came on
    deck sayin', "Fellas, it's too rough t'feed ya."
At seven P.M. a main hatchway caved in;
he said, "Fellas, it's bin good t'know ya!"
The captain wired in he had water comin' in
and the good ship and crew was in peril.
And later that night when 'is lights went outta
    sight came the wreck of the *Edmund Fitzgerald.*

5. Does anyone know where the love of God goes
when the waves turn the minutes to hours?
The searchers all say they'd have made Whitefish
    Bay if they'd put fifteen more miles behind 'er.
They might have split up or they might have
    capsized; they may have broke deep and took water.
And all that remains is the faces and the names
of the wives and the sons and the daughters.

6. Lake Huron rolls, Superior sings
in the rooms of her ice-water mansion.
Old Michigan steams like a young man's dreams;
the islands and bays are for sportsmen.
And farther below Lake Ontario
takes in what Lake Erie can send her,
and the iron boats go as the mariners all know
with the gales of November remembered.

7. In a musty old hall in Detroit they prayed,
In the Maritime Sailors' Cathedral.
The church bell chimed 'til it rang twenty-nine
    times for each man on the *Edmund Fitzgerald.*
The legend lives on from the Chippewa on down
of the big lake they call "Gitchee Gumee."
"Superior," they said, "never gives up her dead
when the gales of November come early!"

Outward Bound

Sailors sang as they worked at their jobs. The shanteyman set the rhythm for the work in his solo. Listen to the recording and join in on the chorus parts when you can.

Rio Grande CD 6-16

Shantey from the United States

Solo
1. Oh say, were you ev - er in Ri - o Grande?
2. A jol - ly good ship and a jol - ly good crew,

Chorus
A - way _____ for Ri - o!

Solo
It's there that the riv - er runs down gold - en sand,
A jol - ly good mate and a jol - ly good crew,

Chorus
We are bound for Ri - o Grande! _____

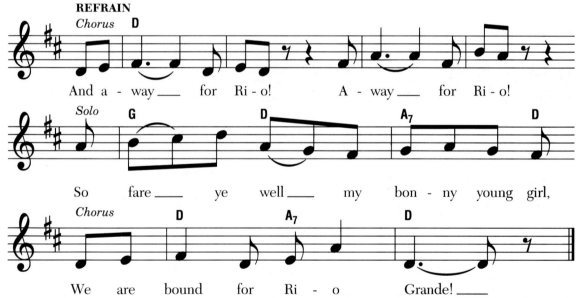

And a - way ___ for Ri - o! A - way ___ for Ri - o!

So fare ___ ye well ___ my bon - ny young girl,

We are bound for Ri - o Grande! ___

3. The anchor's aweigh and the sails they are set, . . .
   The gals that we're leaving we'll never forget, . . .
   Refrain

4. Goodbye to Sally and Sarah and Sue, . . .
   To all who are list'ning, it's goodbye to you, . . .
   Refrain

Haul Up the Anchor

Shanties were the work songs sung aboard sailing ships. Each large sailing ship had a shanteyman—a singer hired for his loud, strong voice, his sense of humor, and his ability to make up verses for any shantey tune.

Cape Cod Shantey

CD 6-17

Sea Shantey from the United States

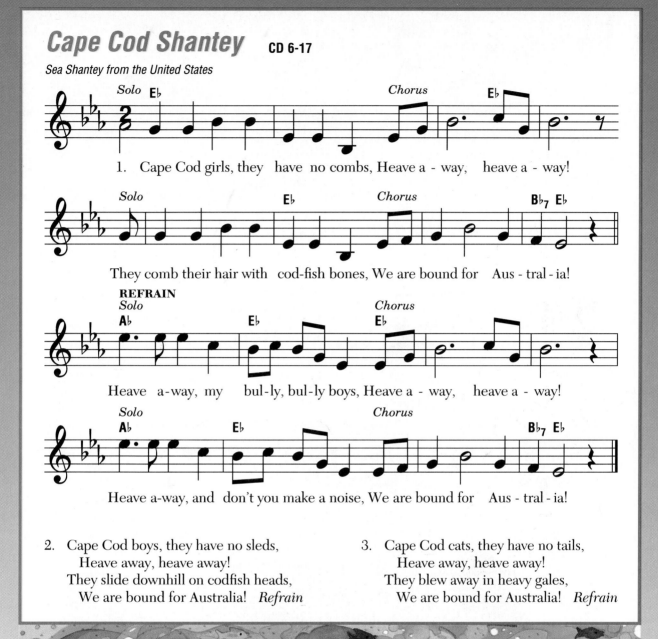

1. Cape Cod girls, they have no combs, Heave a-way, heave a-way!

They comb their hair with cod-fish bones, We are bound for Aus-tral-ia!

REFRAIN

Heave a-way, my bul-ly, bul-ly boys, Heave a-way, heave a-way!

Heave a-way, and don't you make a noise, We are bound for Aus-tral-ia!

2. Cape Cod boys, they have no sleds,
   Heave away, heave away!
   They slide downhill on codfish heads,
   We are bound for Australia! *Refrain*

3. Cape Cod cats, they have no tails,
   Heave away, heave away!
   They blew away in heavy gales,
   We are bound for Australia! *Refrain*

Be a Shanteyman

Make up new verses for the "Cape Cod Shantey" tune. Try using rhymes with fins, tails, gills, and other "fishy" words.

The Roundup

Pretend to sway in the saddle as the cowhand's horse lopes easily along the trail.

Git Along, Little Dogies

CD 6-18

Cowboy Song

1. As I was a-walk-ing one morn-ing for pleas-ure,
2. It's ear-ly in spring that we round up the do-gies,
3. It's whoop-ing and yell-ing and driv-ing the do-gies,

I spied a cow-punch-er a-rid-ing a-lone;
We mark them and brand them and bob off their tails;
And oh, how I wish you would on-ly go on;

His hat was throwed back and his spurs was a-jin-gling,
We round up our hors-es, load up the chuck wag-on,
It's whoop-ing and punch-ing, go on, lit-tle do-gies,

And as he ap-proach'd he was sing-ing this song:
And then throw the do-gies out on-to the trail.
You know that Wy-o-ming will be your new home.

Percussion Accompaniments

Add one of these rhythms to accompany the singing. Autoharp players can follow the chord letters in the music.

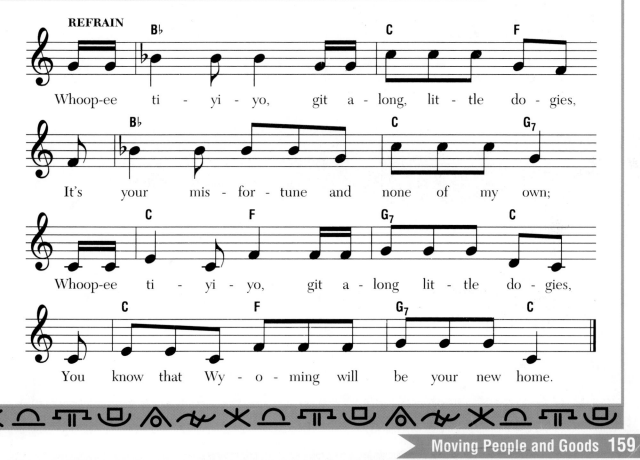

REFRAIN

B♭   C   F

Whoop-ee ti - yi - yo, git a - long, lit - tle do - gies,

B♭   C   G₇

It's your mis - for - tune and none of my own;

C   F   G₇   C

Whoop-ee ti - yi - yo, git a - long lit - tle do - gies,

C   F   G₇   C

You know that Wy - o - ming will be your new home.

ON THE TRAIL

Think about life on the western plains and all the things a cowboy or cowgirl has to do on the job.

I Ride an Old Paint   CD 6-19

Cowboy Song from the United States

1. I ride an old paint and I lead an old dan,
2. Oh, when I die, take my saddle from the wall,

I'm going to Montana for to throw the hoolihan,
Put it on my pony, lead him out of his stall,

They feed in the coulees and water in the draw,
Tie my bones to his back, turn our faces to the west,

Their tails are all matted and their backs are all raw.
And we'll ride the prairies that we love best.

REFRAIN

Get a-long, little dogies, get a-long there slow,

For the fiery and the snuffy are a-rarin' to go.

The Cowboy's Life

The bawl of a steer,
To a cowboy's ear,
    Is music of sweetest strain;
And the yelping notes
Of the gay coyotes
    To him are a glad refrain.

For a kingly crown
In the noisy town
    His saddle he wouldn't change;
No life so free
As the life we see
    Way out on the Yaso range.

The rapid beat
Of his bronco's feet
    On the sod as he speeds along,
Keeps living time
To the ringing rhyme
    Of his rollicking cowboy song.

The winds may blow
And the thunder growl
    Or the breezes may safely moan;
A cowboy's life
Is a royal life,
    His saddle his kingly throne.

John A. Lomax

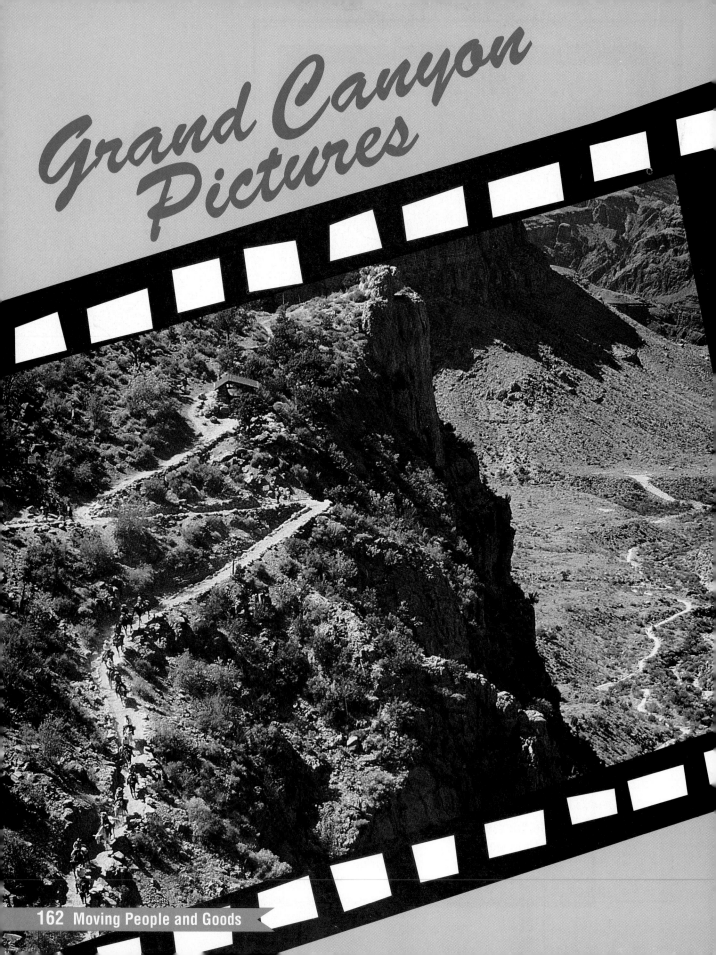

Grand Canyon Pictures

In *The Grand Canyon Suite,* Ferde Grofé presents five pictures of that amazing spectacle of nature. The suite might have been called *A Day in the Grand Canyon* since it follows the sun from rising to setting.

- "Sunrise"
- "The Painted Desert"
- "On the Trail "
- "Sunset"
- "Cloudburst"

You will hear the music from the third and fifth pictures. Before you listen, try to imagine how the music might sound. Then let the photographs help you "picture" each scene as you listen to the music.

 "On the Trail" and "Cloudburst" from
The Grand Canyon Suite ....Ferde Grofé
CD 6-20, 21

THE IRISH HARPER

A bard is a teller of tales and a singer of songs. Follow the words of this song as you listen to the recording. Can you identify the instruments that accompany this gentle Irish tune?

The Bard of Armagh   CD 7-2

Words attributed to Thomas Campbell   Folk Tune from Ireland

1. Oh! List to the tale of a poor Ir - ish har - per,
2. At wake or at fair I would twirl my shi - lay - ly,

And scorn not the strings in his old with - er'd ___ hand;
And trip through a jig with my shoes bound with ___ straw;

But ___ re - mem - ber those fin - gers could ___ once move much sharp - er,
And ___ all the ___ pret - ty maid - ens from ___ vil - lage and val - ley,

To wa - ken the ech - oes of his dear na - tive land.
Love the bold Phel - im Bra - dy, the ___ bard of Ar - magh.

Boltin Picture Library

Sounds of Ireland ....
.... Traditional

CD 7-3

When you can sing "The Bard of Armagh" without the recording, follow the chord names in the music and play your own harp-like accompaniment on the autoharp.

How Songs Travel

When Irish immigrants came to the United States toward the middle of the last century, they brought many of their songs with them. And they changed some of their old songs to suit their new life. In America, "The Bard of Armagh" was transformed into the popular cowboy song called "Streets of Laredo." You will find the words of "Streets of Laredo" on page 281 in your book. Follow this story-song as you listen to the recording.

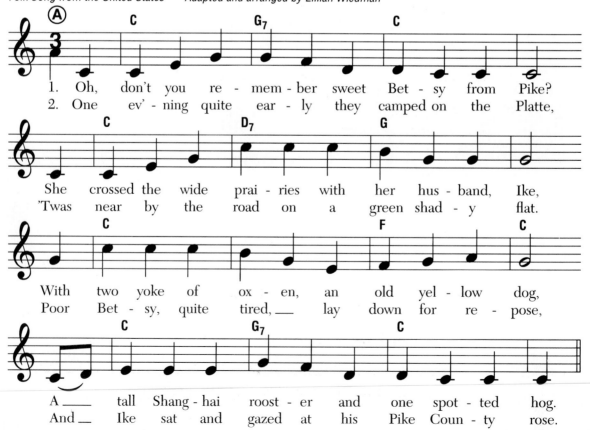

Across the Wide Prairies

Imagine what it must have been like to travel across the country in a covered wagon in the year 1849. You would have needed more than a sense of humor to do it!

Sweet Betsy from Pike   CD 7-6

Folk Song from the United States   *Adapted and arranged by Lillian Wiedman*

1. Oh, don't you re-mem-ber sweet Bet-sy from Pike?
2. One ev'-ning quite ear-ly they camped on the Platte,

She crossed the wide prai-ries with her hus-band, Ike,
'Twas near by the road on a green shad-y flat.

With two yoke of ox-en, an old yel-low dog,
Poor Bet-sy, quite tired, __ lay down for re-pose,

A __ tall Shang-hai roost-er and one spot-ted hog.
And __ Ike sat and gazed at his Pike Coun-ty rose.

REFRAIN

Too - ra - lee, too - ra - lay,

Too - ra - lee, too - ra - lay,

Sing-ing too - ra - lee, too - ra - lee, too - ra - lee ay.

3. They soon reached the desert where Betsy gave out.
And down on the sand she lay rolling about.
While Ike, in great tears, looked on in surprise:
Said, "Betsy, get up, you'll get sand in your eyes." *Refrain*

4. The rooster ran off and the oxen all died:
The last piece of bacon that morning was fried.
Poor Ike got discouraged and Betsy got mad:
The dog wagged his tail and looked awfully sad. *Refrain*

5. The alkali desert was burning and hot,
And Ike, he decided to leave on the spot:
"My dear old Pike County, I'll go back to you."
Said Betsy, "You'll go by yourself if you do." *Refrain*

6. They swam the wide rivers, they crossed the tall peaks,
They camped out on prairies for weeks and for weeks,
Fought hunger and rattlers and big storms of dust,
Determined to reach California or bust. *Refrain*

New Words for Old Tunes

"Sweet Betsy from Pike" is an example of a new song made from an old tune. The old tune was an English ballad that began:

A wealthy old merchant in London did dwell.
He had a young daughter, an uncommon fine gal.

People are always adding new words to old folk tunes. Can you think of a new verse to add to this old story of Betsy and Ike?

AN AMERICAN NONSENSE SONG

"Clementine" crossed the country with prospectors heading for the California gold fields. On the long journey, the forty-niners sang the tunes that were popular back home and made up their own nonsense words, which helped them to laugh at their hardships.

Clementine

CD 7-7

Folk Song from the United States

1. In a cav-ern by a can-yon, Ex-ca-vat-ing for a mine,
2. Light she was and like a feath-er, And her shoes were num-ber nine,

Dwelt a min-er, for-ty-nin-er, And his daugh-ter, Clem-en-tine.
Her-ring box-es with-out top-ses, San-dals were for Clem-en-tine.

REFRAIN

Oh, my dar-lin', oh, my dar-lin', Oh, my dar-lin' Clem-en-tine,

You are lost and gone for-ev-er, Dread-ful sor-ry, Clem-en-tine.

3. Drove she ducklings to the water
   Every morning just at nine;
   Struck her foot against a splinter,
   Fell into the foaming brine. *Refrain*

4. Rosy lips above the water
   Blowing bubbles mighty fine;
   But, alas! I was no swimmer,
   So I lost my Clementine. *Refrain*

Make up your own nonsense words for "Clementine" and practice this chord pattern on the autoharp. Then sing your new words and play your own accompaniment.

This cowhand sings about leaving
home and hitting the trail for Mexico.

Old Texas   CD 7-8

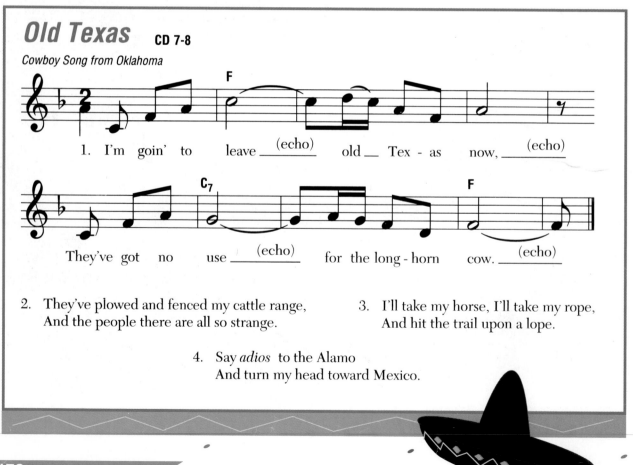

Cowboy Song from Oklahoma

F

1. I'm goin' to leave ___ (echo) old __ Tex - as now, ___ (echo)

C₇   **F**

They've got no use ___ (echo) for the long - horn cow. ___ (echo)

2. They've plowed and fenced my cattle range,
   And the people there are all so strange.

3. I'll take my horse, I'll take my rope,
   And hit the trail upon a lope.

4. Say *adios* to the Alamo
   And turn my head toward Mexico.

The melody of "Old Texas" was a favorite in the Old West. Many different sets of words were sung to the same tune. Try putting these words to the "Old Texas" tune.

O bury me not on the lone prairie
Where the coyotes howl and the wind blows free,
Where the buffalo roams o'er a prairie sea,
O bury me not on the lone prairie.

Metropolitan Museum of Art, New York

Steers at Play   *Lawrence H. Lebduska*

STEPHEN FOSTER'S HIT SONG

The banjo was a popular folk instrument in Stephen Foster's time. Listen for its sound on this recording of "Oh, Susanna."

Oh, Susanna CD 7-9

Words and Music by Stephen Foster

1. I ___ came from Al - a - ba - ma With my ban - jo on my knee,
2. I ___ had a dream the oth - er night, When ev - 'ry-thing was still,

I'm ___ going to Loui - si - an - a, My ___ true love for to see;
I ___ thought I saw Su - san - na A - com - ing down the hill.

It ___ rained all night the day I left, The weath-er it was dry;
The ___ buck-wheat cake was in her mouth, The tear was in her eye.

The ___ sun so hot I froze to death; Su - san - na, don't you cry.
Says ___ I, "I'm com - ing from the South, Su - san - na, don't you cry."

REFRAIN

Oh, Su - san - na, Oh, don't you cry for me,

I've _ come from Al - a - ba - ma With my ban - jo on my knee.

Of all the songs that Stephen Foster wrote, "Oh, Susanna" is the best-known and best-loved. Foster wrote "Oh, Susanna" for a small singing society that he conducted. Later it became the favorite song of the "forty-niners" when they traveled to California's goldfields. Here are the words they sang.

> I soon shall be in Frisco,
> And there I'll look around,
> And when I see the gold lumps there
> I'll pick them off the ground.
> I'll scrape the mountains clean, my boys,
> I'll drain the rivers dry,
> A pocketful of rocks bring home—
> So brothers don't you cry.
>
> Oh, California,
> That's the land for me!
> I'm bound for San Francisco
> With my washbowl on my knee.

On this recording you will hear two different singing groups performing "Oh, Susanna" in two different styles.

CD 7-10

Oh, Susanna (The Byrds)
.....................Stephen Foster

CD 7-11

Oh, Susanna (The Mormon Tabernacle Choir)
.....................Stephen Foster

Voices of the World

Follow the words of this poem as you listen to the recording.

CD 7-12

Voices of the World

There is music
in the hearts of people—
the music of joy
turned into song—
a roundelay of happiness—
lifting all voices
in one choir
of the world.

There is a dance-step
to the heart-beat of people—
a timing of gladness—
of nimble feet
and clapping hands—
widening around
the magic circle
of the world.

There is music
in the gypsy-tune
of violins—
a piper's flute—
the roll of an organ chord—
a tinkling chime—

the drum-beat
of a town-band on parade . .

Music is the sound of life awakening
The voices of the world.

Stefi Samuelson

Springtime in Korea

In the springtime, young girls gather the edible roots of the *Doraji* plant that grows in the hills and valleys.

Bluebells *(Doraji)* CD 7-13, 14

Folk Song from Korea   *Collected and translated by Patricia Shehan Campbell*

Blue - bells, blue - bells, Love - ly blue - bells,
Do - ra - ji, do - ra - ji, pek do - ra - ji,

Deep in the moun - tains __ my __ blue - bells grow.
Sim - sim ___ san - chuh __ oh ___ pek do - ra - ji.

Gath - er - ing blue - bells in wide val - leys.
Hahn ___ du bu - ri - man keh - yuh - do _____

Bas - kets of ___ blue - bells __ will __ o - ver - flow.
Teh kwang-chu - ri su - ri - sal ___ sal ___ dah - nuh - nun - da.

from the Coast of Colombia

This humorous song tells about an alligator who has bread and cheese and cold lemonade for dinner.

The Alligator (Se va el caimán)

CD 7-15, 16

English words by Aura Kontra   Dance Song from Colombia

Let me tell a sil - ly sto - ry ___ on a light and hap - py note, __
Voy a_em-pe-zar mi re-la - to ___ con a - le-gría y con a fán. ___

Let me tell a sil - ly sto - ry ___ on a light and hap - py note. _
Voy a_em-pe-zar mi re-la - to ___ con a - le-gría y con a fán, ___

On the riv - er Mag - da - le - na, ___ a ga - tor likes to float, _
Por el rí - o Mag - da - le - na ___ se vol - vió_un hom-bre cai - mán, _

On the riv - er Mag - da - le - na, ___ a ga - tor likes to float.
Por el rí - o Mag - da - le - na ___ se vol - vió_un hom-bre cai - mán.

REFRAIN

Oh, there he goes, oh, there he goes;
He's leav-ing for Ba-rran-qui - lla;
Se va el cai - mán, se va el cai - mán,
Se va pa-ra Ba-rran-qui - lla,

1.

Oh, there he goes, oh, there he goes;
He's leav-ing for Ba-rran-qui - lla.
Se va el cai - mán, se va el cai - mán,
Se va pa-ra Ba-rran-qui - lla.

2. to verses 2 and 3   last time

leav-ing for Ba-rran-qui - lla.
leav-ing for Ba-rran-qui - lla.
va pa-ra Ba-rran-qui - lla.
va pa-ra Ba-rran-qui - lla.

2. What this gator has for dinner
      is a wonder to behold, *(2 times)*
    There is cheese and there is bread
      and lemonade served cold. *(2 times)*
    Refrain

3. On the far side of the river,
      fishermen reeled in a perch, *(2 times)*
    It had swallowed the guitarist,
      now they've called off the search. *(2 times)*
    Refrain

2. *Lo que come este caimán
      yo le tengo admiración,* *(2 times)*
    *Come queso y come pan
      con refrescos de limón.* *(2 times)*
    Refrain

3. *Al otro lado del río
      pescaron una mojarra,* *(2 times)*
    *Y del buche le sacaron
      él que toca la guitarra.* *(2 times)*
    Refrain

Boys and girls who live in Africa learn the customs of their people through singing and dancing. The Onchimbo bird is a symbol of a certain group, and in this song the singers are asking a favor from the bird.

Onchimbo CD 7-17

English Words by Margaret Marks   *African Folk Song from Kenya*   *As sung by Ruth Nthreketha*

Leader

O take your fair share, — good fish-ing / good hunt-ing On-chim-bo bird.

Chorus

O take your fair share, — good fish-ing / good hunt-ing On-chim-bo bird.

Leader

Take fish from the stream, — good fish-ing / good hunt-ing On-chim-bo bird.
Take game from the plain, — good fish-ing / good hunt-ing

Chorus

Take fish from the stream, — good fish-ing / good hunt-ing On-chim-bo bird.
Take game from the plain, — good fish-ing / good hunt-ing

When you can sing the song, play a percussion part on the top of your desk or on a drum.

Waninamba Council Drum

African Proverbs

Do you know a proverb that has the same meaning as one of these?

• If you climb up a tree, you must climb down the same tree.

• The horse that arrives early gets good drinking water.

• By trying often, the monkey learns to jump from the tree.

• Little by little grow the bananas.

Listen to the drummers on this recording.

Drum Duet
............Malenka Tribe

CD 7-18

Bell Parts

Animals in Music

Think of all the songs you know that talk about animals. Many composers have painted musical pictures of animals. On this recording you will hear six pieces of music. Can you match each musical description with one of the animals listed below? Can you give reasons for your choices?

Musical Animals

CD 7-22

cat	bee
chick	lion
mosquito	donkey

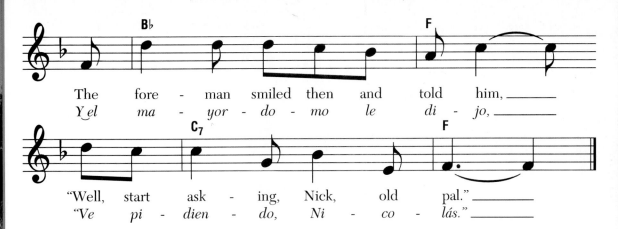

The fore - man smiled then and told him, _____
Y el ma - yor - do - mo le di - jo, _____

"Well, start ask - ing, Nick, old pal." _____
"Ve pi - dien - do, Ni - co - lás." _____

2. "I need some thirty *pesos,*
A jacket, coat, and a hat."
The foreman smiled then and told him,
"No money have I for that."
"I need those thirty *pesos*
For to marry my sweet gal."
The foreman smiled then and told him,
"I have none, my dear, old pal."

2. "*Necesito treinta pesos,*
Una cuera y un gabán."
Y el mayordomo le dijo,
"*No hay dinero, Nicolás.*"
"*Necesito treinta pesos*
Para poderme casar."
Y el mayordomo le dijo,
"*Ni un real tengo, Nicolás.*"

El siquisirí
.... Folk Song From Mexico
CD 7-25

A Chinese Lullaby

"Bamboo Flute" is a very old Chinese lullaby. It is sung by village mothers to their children.

The poetry of ancient China contains lines of rare beauty. Tu Fu, (712-770) one of China's greatest poets, captured the beauty of nature in his poetry. Try reading this poem aloud.

Clear Evening after Rain

The sun sinks toward the horizon.
The light clouds are blown away.
A rainbow shines on the river.
The last raindrops spatter the rocks.
Cranes and herons soar in the sky.
Fat bears feed along the banks.
I wait here for the west wind
And enjoy the crescent moon
Shining through misty bamboos.

Tu Fu (712-770)

Bamboo Flute   (Hsiao)   CD 7-26

Folk Song from China

From   the   pur - ple   straight   bam - boo;
Yi   geng   zi   zhu   zhi   miao   miao;
yee   gong   dzuh   joo   jüh   mee ow   mee ow

I   have   made   a   flute   for   you.
Sung   yu   bao   bao   zuo   guan   xiao.
sohng   yu   bow   bow   tsoo oh   gwahn   shee ow

Take   the   bam - boo   flute,   Put   it   to   your   lips,
Xiao   er   dui   zheng   kou   Kou   er   dui   zheng   xiao;
shee ow   er   dweh   jeng   koh   koh   er   dweh   jeng   shee ow

Play   a   new   and   lilt - ing   song.
Xiao   zhong   chui   chu   shi   xin   diao;
shee ow   jung   chway   choo   shee   shehn   dow

My   lit - tle   one,   Play   a   new and   lilt - ing   song,
Xiao   bao   bao   Yi   di   yi   di   xue   hui   liao,
shee ow   bow   bow   yee   dee   yee   dee   shau   hwī   lee ow

My   lit - tle   one,   Play a   new and   lilt - ing   song.
Xiao   bao   bao   Yi   di   yi   di   xue hui   liao.
shee ow   bow   bow   yee dee   yee   dee shau hwī   lee ow

A Special Sound from Japan

The koto is one of the most popular instruments in Japan. Listen for its special sound on the recording of "Sakura."

Sakura CD 7-27

English Version by Lorene Hoyt   Folk Song from Japan   Modern Arrangement by Henry Burnett

1. Sa - ku - ra, Sa - ku - ra, Cher - ry blos - soms
2. Sa - ku - ra, Sa - ku - ra, Blos - soms wav - ing
   Sa - ku - ra, Sa - ku - ra, Ya - yo - i no

ev - 'ry - where. Clouds of glo - ry fill the __ sky,
in the __ breeze. Yo - shi - no, the cher - ry __ land,
so - ra __ wa, Mi - wa - ta - su ka - gi - ri,

Mist of beau - ty in the __ air, Love - ly col - ors float - ing __ by,
Tat - su - ta, the ma - ple __ trees, Ka - ra - sa - ki, pine tree __ grand,
Ka - su - mi ka ku - mo - ka, Ni - o - i zo i - zu - ru;

Sa - ku - ra, Sa - ku - ra, Let __ all come __ sing - ing.
Sa - ku - ra, Sa - ku - ra, Let __ all come __ sing - ing.
i - za - ya, i - za - ya Mi __ ni yu - kan. ____

Countermelody for bells or recorder

On this recording you will hear a master musician perform "Sakura" on the koto.

CD 7-28 *Sakura* from *Japanese Masterpieces for the Koto*

TAGALOG FOLK SONG

This humorous song from the Philippines is about a boy named Leron who climbed a papaya tree to get some fruit for his sweetheart. This was a foolish thing to do because everybody in the Pacific Islands knows that the papaya branches won't support a person's weight! The fruit must be gotten down by shaking the tree or using a pole.

Leron, Leron   CD 7-29

Folk Song from the Philippines

1. Le - ron, Le - ron, my boy, be care - ful what you do,
2. Le - ron, Le - ron, my boy, climbed up pa - pa - ya tree,
Le - ron, Le - ron, sin - ta Bu - ko ng pa - pa - ya,

The tall pa - pa - ya tree is far too high for you.
A bas - ket in his hand to fill with love for me.
Da la - da - lá'y bus - lo, Si - sid - lan ng sin - ta,

The trunk is much too thin, the branch - es are too small,
The top - most branch he touched, it broke off with a "click,"
Peg - da - ting sa du - la'y Na - ba - li ang sa - nga,

So bring your bas - ket down be - fore you get a fall.
A - las, Le - ron my boy, please choose an - oth - er quick!
Ka - pos ka - pa - la - ran, Hu - ma - na o ng i - ba.

An Asian Chant

Follow the music of "Shri Ram, Jai Ram" as you listen to the recording of this chant from India.

Shri Ram, Jai Ram   CD 7-30

Hindu Chant

Leader Shri Ram, jai Ram, jai jai Ram, **Group** Shri Ram, jai Ram, jai jai Ram,

Leader Shri Ram, jai Ram, jai jai Ram, **Group** Shri Ram, jai Ram, jai jai Ram,

Leader Shri Ram, jai Ram, jai jai Ram, _ **Group** Shri Ram, jai Ram, jai jai Ram _

1.

2. jai Ram, jai jai Ram, _ **Leader** Shri Ram, jai Ram, jai jai Ram,

Group Shri Ram, jai Ram, jai jai Ram. **All** Shan - ti, Shan - ti, Shan - ti.

As sung by Amrit Barush, From East-West songs, Courtesy of World Around Songs, Inc.

Try singing the C scale, using the Indian names. Then make up your own leader-group song, using only the notes C, D, E, G, and A.

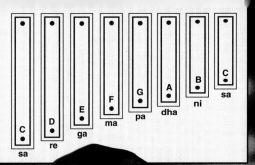

| C | D | E | F | G | A | B | C |
| sa | re | ga | ma | pa | dha | ni | sa |

This photograph shows Ravi Shankar playing a sitar. He is one of the best-known sitarists in the world.

CD 8-1

The Sounds of India

East, West, North, and South

What does the title "Common Ground" mean to you?
Follow the words of the song as you listen to the recording.

Common Ground   CD 8-2, 3

Words and Music by Michael Bacon

1. Vill - age _ in _ New Eng - land   is   blank - et - ed _ with snow.
   School bus _ in _ Mon - tan - a _____   drives the o - pen range.

   While in Cal - i - for - nia,   av - o - ca - dos grow.
   Teach - er in _ Man - hat - tan   rides the sub - way train.

   Storm - in' _ on _ Lake E - rie.   Fair in Pu - get Sound.
   White sails _ in _ the breez - es   on Long Is - land Sound.

   in this land _ of diff - 'ren - ces, _ we're the com - mon ground.

2. We're the com - mon ground.   The world is not so wide _

   When we're stand - ing side by side. _____   Lift - ing up our voic - es.   Our

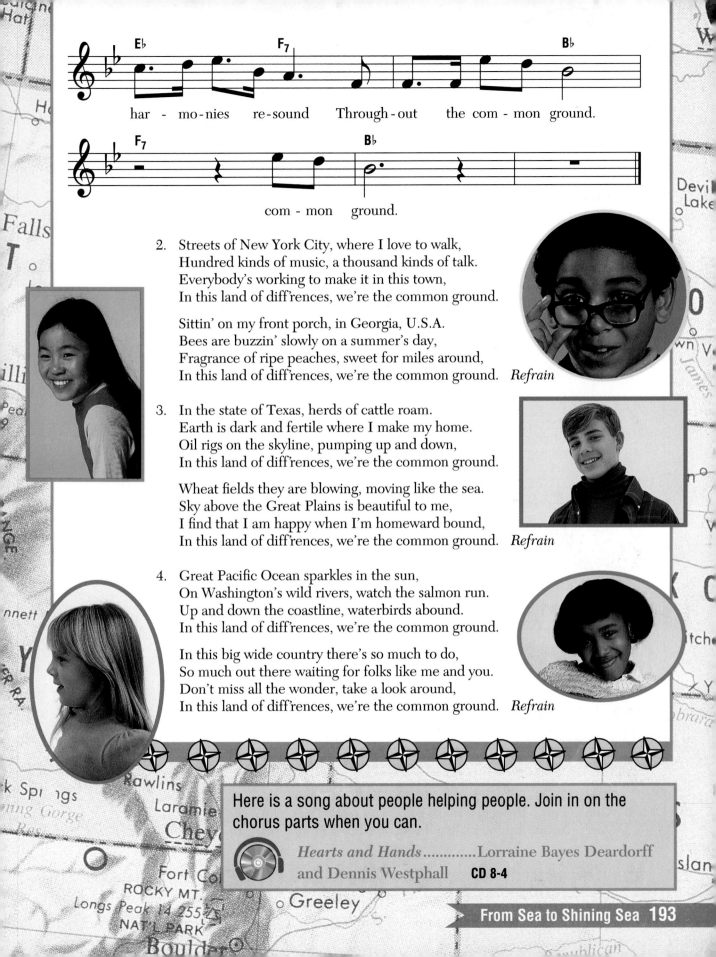

har - mo - nies re-sound Through-out the com - mon ground.

com - mon ground.

2. Streets of New York City, where I love to walk,
Hundred kinds of music, a thousand kinds of talk.
Everybody's working to make it in this town,
In this land of diff'rences, we're the common ground.

Sittin' on my front porch, in Georgia, U.S.A.
Bees are buzzin' slowly on a summer's day,
Fragrance of ripe peaches, sweet for miles around,
In this land of diff'rences, we're the common ground. *Refrain*

3. In the state of Texas, herds of cattle roam.
Earth is dark and fertile where I make my home.
Oil rigs on the skyline, pumping up and down,
In this land of diff'rences, we're the common ground.

Wheat fields they are blowing, moving like the sea.
Sky above the Great Plains is beautiful to me,
I find that I am happy when I'm homeward bound,
In this land of diff'rences, we're the common ground. *Refrain*

4. Great Pacific Ocean sparkles in the sun,
On Washington's wild rivers, watch the salmon run.
Up and down the coastline, waterbirds abound.
In this land of diff'rences, we're the common ground.

In this big wide country there's so much to do,
So much out there waiting for folks like me and you.
Don't miss all the wonder, take a look around,
In this land of diff'rences, we're the common ground. *Refrain*

Here is a song about people helping people. Join in on the chorus parts when you can.

Hearts and Hands..............Lorraine Bayes Deardorff and Dennis Westphall   **CD 8-4**

From Sea to Shining Sea

On a beautiful day in 1893, Katharine Lee Bates stood on the top of Colorado's Pikes Peak and looked for miles in every direction. She seemed to be seeing all of America—mountains, valleys, wide prairies. It was after this experience that she wrote the poem "America, the Beautiful."

America, the Beautiful   CD 8-5

Words by Katharine Lee Bates   Music by Samuel A. Ward

1. O beau-ti-ful for spa-cious skies, For am-ber waves of grain,
2. O beau-ti-ful for Pil-grim feet, Whose stern im-pas-sioned stress
3. O beau-ti-ful for pa-triot dream That sees be-yond the years

For pur-ple moun-tain maj-es-ties A-bove the fruit-ed plain!
A thor-ough-fare for free-dom beat A-cross the wil-der-ness!
Thine al-a-bas-ter cit-ies gleam, Un-dimmed by hu-man tears!

A-mer-i-ca! A-mer-i-ca! God shed His grace on thee
A-mer-i-ca! A-mer-i-ca! God mend thine ev-'ry flaw,
A-mer-i-ca! A-mer-i-ca! God shed His grace on thee

And crown thy good with broth-er-hood From sea to shin-ing sea!
Con-firm thy soul in self con-trol, Thy lib-er-ty in law!
And crown thy good with broth-er-hood From sea to shin-ing sea!

Katharine Lee Bates

What can you discover about the phrases in this song? The first phrase is shown in a color box.

Countermelody for Bells or Recorder

Sweet Land of Liberty

The words of "America" are set to a melody that has been around for many years. No one knows where the tune came from, but many people have used it—the Germans, the Swiss, the French. Great Britain's national anthem has the same melody.

A Nation's Strength

Not gold, but only man can make
A people great and strong;
Men who, for truth and honor's sake,
Stand fast and suffer long.
Brave men who work while others sleep,
Who dare while others fly—
They build a nation's pillars deep
And lift them to the sky.

Ralph Waldo Emerson

America   CD 8-7

Words by Samuel Francis Smith   *Traditional Melody*

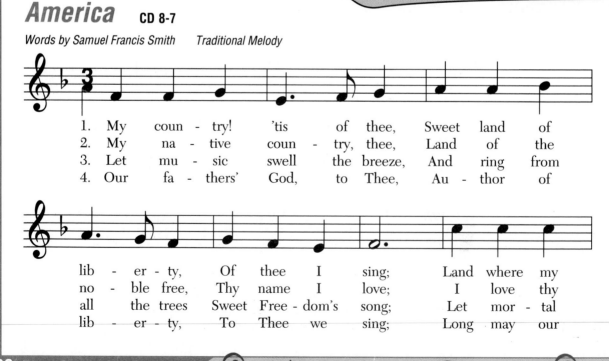

1. My coun - try! 'tis of thee, Sweet land of
2. My na - tive coun - try, thee, Land of the
3. Let mu - sic swell the breeze, And ring from
4. Our fa - thers' God, to Thee, Au - thor of

lib - er - ty, Of thee I sing; Land where my
no - ble free, Thy name I love; I love thy
all the trees Sweet Free - dom's song; Let mor - tal
lib - er - ty, To Thee we sing; Long may our

John Szoke Graphics, Inc., New York

Charles Ives, an American composer, used the melody of "America" in one of his compositions. Listen to Ives' *Variations on "America,"* arranged for symphony orchestra.

Variations on "America"
....................Charles Ives

CD 8-8

Statue of Liberty   *James Rizzi*

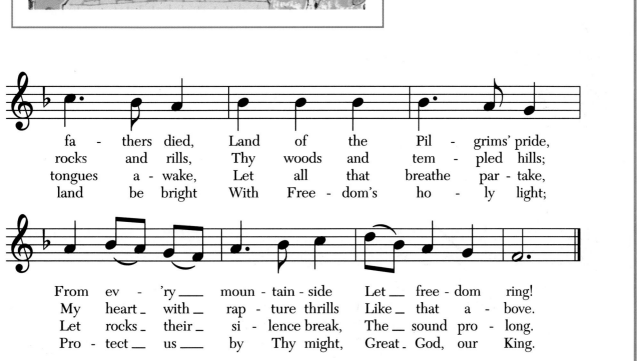

fa - thers died,	Land	of	the	Pil - grims' pride,
rocks and rills,	Thy	woods and	tem - pled hills;
tongues a - wake,	Let	all	that	breathe par - take,
land be bright	With	Free - dom's	ho - ly light;

From ev - 'ry __ moun - tain - side	Let __ free - dom ring!
My heart _ with _ rap - ture thrills	Like _ that a - bove.
Let rocks _ their _ si - lence break,	The _ sound pro - long.
Pro - tect _ us __ by Thy might,	Great _ God, our King.

A Freedom Song

"We Shall Overcome" is a famous freedom song. It is based on a Southern hymn. During the Civil War, the Union soldiers sang it. Now it is a musical symbol of the civil rights movement and of the work of Martin Luther King, Jr.

Chant and Play

Follow the rhythm score below as you listen to this recording.

Martin Luther King Chant ....
Randy DeLelles and Jeff Kriske
CD 8-11

We Shall Overcome CD 8-9, 10

Freedom Song from the United States
New Words and Arrangement by Zilphia Horton, Frank Hamilton, Guy Carawan, and Pete Seeger

1. We shall o-ver-come, _____ We shall o-ver-come, _____
2. We'll walk hand in hand. _____ We'll walk hand in hand, _____
3. We are not a-fraid, _____ We are not a-fraid, _____
4. We shall broth-ers be, _____ We shall broth-ers be, _____
5. Truth shall make us free, _____ Truth shall make us free, _____

We shall o-ver-come some-day; _____
We'll walk hand in hand some-day; _____
We are not a-fraid to-day; _____
We shall broth-ers be some-day; _____
Truth shall make us free some-day; _____

Oh, ___ deep in my heart I do be-lieve,
Oh, ___ deep in my heart I do be-lieve,
Oh, ___ deep in my heart I do be-lieve,
Oh, ___ deep in my heart I do be-lieve,
Oh, ___ deep in my heart I do be-lieve,

(last time)

We shall o-ver-come some-day. _____
We shall o-ver-come some-day. _____
We shall o-ver-come some-day. _____
We shall o-ver-come some-day. _____
We shall o-ver-come some-day. _____

The Flag is Passing By

Play a drum beat on your desk as you listen to the music of "You're a Grand Old Flag."

You're a Grand Old Flag

CD 8-12

Words and Music by George M. Cohan

You're a grand old flag, you're a high-fly-ing flag;

And for-ev-er in peace may you wave; _____

You're the em-blem of the land I love,

The home of the free and the brave. _____

Ev-'ry heart beats true un-der red, white, and blue,

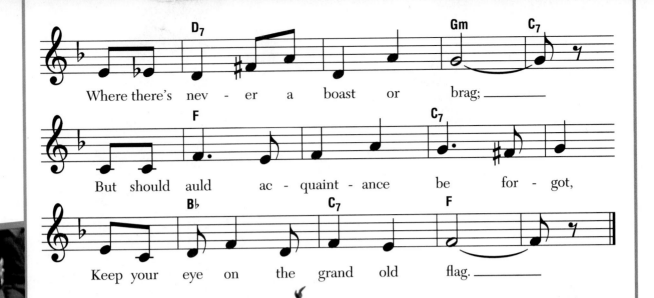

Where there's nev - er a boast or brag; _____

But should auld ac - quaint - ance be for - got,

Keep your eye on the grand old flag. _____

The Flag Goes By

Hats off!
Along the street there comes
A blare of bugles, a ruffle of drums,
A flash of color beneath the sky:
Hats off!
The flag is passing by!
Hats off!
Along the street there comes
A blare of bugles, a ruffle of drums;
And loyal hearts are beating high:
Hats off!
The flag is passing by!

Henry Holcomb Bennett

Our National Anthem

"The Star-Spangled Banner" is performed on many occasions. On what occasions might you hear or sing the national anthem?

The Star-Spangled Banner   CD 8-13

Words by Francis Scott Key   Music by John Stafford Smith

Oh, __ say! can you see, by the dawn's ear - ly light,

What so proud - ly we hailed at the twi - light's last gleam-ing,

Whose broad stripes and bright stars, through the per - il - ous fight,

O'er the ram - parts we watched were so gal - lant - ly stream-ing?

The composer used three favorite parade tunes in this piano piece. If you listen very carefully, you may be able to identify one of the tunes.

"July" from *A Calendar Set*
Judith Lang Zaimont

CD 8-14

And the rock - ets' red glare, the bombs burst - ing in air,

Gave proof through the night that our flag was still there.

Oh, say, does that __ Star-Span-gled Ban - ner __ yet __ wave __

O'er the land __ of the free and the home of the brave?

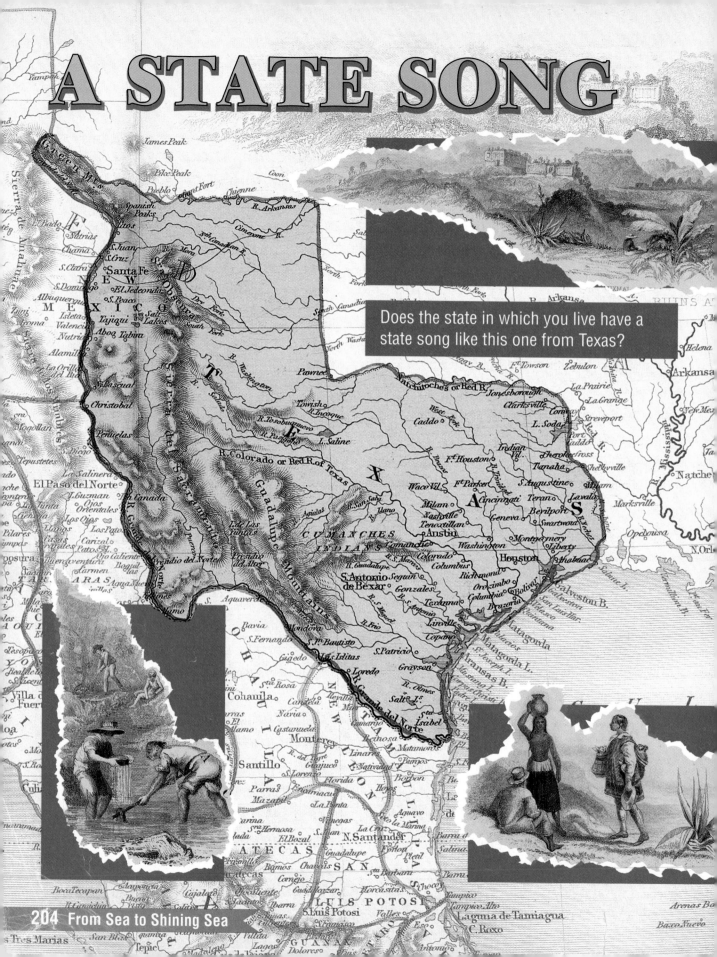

A STATE SONG

Does the state in which you live have a state song like this one from Texas?

Texas, Our Texas CD 8-15

Words by Gladys Yoakum Wright and William J. Marsh   *Music by William J. Marsh*

1. Tex - as, our Tex - as! All hail the might - y state!
2. Tex - as, O Tex - as! your free-born sin - gle star
3. Tex - as, dear Tex - as! From ty - rant grip now free.

Tex - as, our Tex - as! So won - der - ful, so great!
Sends out its ra - diance to na - tions near and far.
Shines forth in splen - dor your star of des - ti - ny!

Bold - est and grand - est, With - stand - ing ev - 'ry test;
Em - blem of free - dom! It sets our hearts a - glow
Moth - er of he - roes! We come, your chil - dren true.

O Em - pire wide and glo - rious, You stand su - preme-ly blest.
With thoughts of San Ja - cin - to and glo - rious A - la - mo.
Pro - claim - ing our al - le - giance, Our faith, our love for you.

REFRAIN

God bless you, Tex - as! And keep you brave and strong,

That you may grow in pow'r and worth, Through-out the ag - es long.

God bless you, Tex - as! And keep you brave and strong,

That you may grow in pow'r and worth, Through-out the ag - es long.

It's Halloween!

Think of ways of using your voice to make this Halloween song exciting.

Halloween   CD 8-16

Words and Music by John Horman

1. You got-ta watch out ___ when the ghosts come round, ___

You got-ta watch out ___ so you won't be found, ___

'Cause if they should find you and sneak up be-hind you,

You got-ta watch out ___ when the ghosts come round. ___

2. You gotta watch out when the moon is high,
And witches ride broomsticks across the sky,
For if they should spy you and fly down beside you,
You gotta watch out when the moon is high.

3. When Halloween comes around this year,
And spooky things fill your heart with fear,
Remember, be wary of things that are scary,
When Halloween comes around this year.

Hallowe'en

Tonight is the night
When dead leaves fly
Like witches on switches
Across the sky.
When elf and sprite
Flit through the night
On a moony sheen.

Tonight is the night
When leaves make a sound
Like a gnome in his home
Under the ground,
When the spooks and trolls
Creep out of holes
Mossy and green.

Tonight is the night
When pumpkins stare
Through the sheaves and leaves
Everywhere,
When ghoul and ghost
And goblin host
Dance around their queen.
It's Hallowe'en!

Harry Behn

Ghosts and Goblins

Watch Out!   CD 8-17

Words and Music by John Horman

When ghosts and gob - lins come to town, —

And skel - e - tons all dance a - round, —

Just pull those cov - ers o - ver your head and

1. then, —   2. then, — watch out!

© 1984 John Horman

Halloween Chant

Ghosts,   Ghosts

Gob - lins,   Gob - lins

Skel - e - tons,   Skel - e - tons

Ooh _____

Partner Songs for Halloween

You got - ta watch out ___ when the ghosts come round, ___ You

When ghosts and gob - lins come to town, ___ And

got - ta watch out ___ so you won't be found, ___ 'Cause

skel - e - tons all dance a - round, ___ Just

if they should find you and sneak up be - hind you, You

pull those co - vers o - ver your head and

got - ta watch out ___ when the ghosts come round. ___

then, _____ watch out!

HARVEST FESTIVAL

Sukkot is an autumn festival. It comes at the time of year when farmers cut down their full-grown wheat and get ready for the long winter.

Harvest Time (Ha' Sukkah)   CD 8-18

English Words by Lillian Wiedman   Hebrew Folk Song

1. Cut the wheat, gold-en wheat, Oh, how beau-ti-ful the har-vest;
2. Pluck the grapes, pur-ple grapes, Oh, how beau-ti-ful the har-vest;
   Ha' Suk-kah, mah ya-fah u-mah tov la-she-vet bah! ___

Cut the wheat, gold-en wheat, Oh, how beau-ti-ful it is!
Pluck the grapes, pur-ple grapes, Oh, how beau-ti-ful they are!
Ha' Suk-kah, mah ya-fah u-mah tov la-she-vet bah!

Used by permission of Board of Jewish Education

The First Thanksgiving

The Pilgrims' first Thanksgiving feast took place in mid-October 1621. They were so thankful for their survival and their plentiful harvest of Indian corn that they decided to set aside a day for giving thanks. The day was filled with prayer, feasting, and merriment.

We Gather Together   CD 8-21

English Words by Theodore Baker   *Traditional Tune from the Netherlands*

p
1. We gath-er to-geth-er to ask the Lord's bless-ing;

mf
2. Be-side us to guide us, our God with us join-ing,

f
3. We all do ex-tol Thee, Thou lead-er tri-um-phant,

He chas-tens and has-tens His will to make known.
Or-dain-ing, main-tain-ing His king-dom di-vine.
And pray that Thou still our de-fend-er wilt be.

The wick-ed op-press-ing, now cease from dis-tress-ing.
So from the be-gin-ning, the fight we were win-ning.
Let Thy con-gre-ga-tion es-cape trib-u-la-tion.

Sing prais-es to His name; He for-gets not His own.
Thou, Lord, wast at our side; All glo-ry be Thine.
Thy name be ev-er prais-ed! O Lord, make us free!

Winter Fantasy

CD 8-22, 23

Words and Music by Jill Gallina

Part I

Snow-flakes fall - ing all o - ver town, slip - ping slid - ing
There's an i - cy chill in the air, tell - ing us that

1. ev - 'ry-bod - y rush - in' 'round.
2. win - ter's real - ly here. Oh!

I'm so glad that win - ter is here. Grab your sled and

let out a hap-py cheer be-cause it's snow-ing, blow-ing, all through the day.

Win - ter winds will sure - ly blow all your cares a - way.

Part II

Dash-ing thru the snow in a one-horse o-pen sleigh. O'er the fields we go

There are two different melodies in "Winter Fantasy."
Create harmony by singing the melodies as partner songs.

Laugh-ing all the way. Bells on bob-tails ring, mak-ing spir-its bright.

What fun it is to laugh and sing a sleigh-ing song to-night. Oh!

Jin - gle bells, jin - gle bells, jin - gle all the way.

Oh, what fun it is to ride in a one-horse o - pen sleigh. __

Jin - gle bells, jin - gle bells, jin - gle all the way.

Oh, what fun it is to ride in a one-horse o - pen sleigh.

Ringing Bells

Listen for the echo part in the recording of this song. In which section do you hear it—section A or section B?

Silver Bells   CD 8-24, 25

Words and Music by Jay Livingston and Ray Evans

A

B♭   E♭

1. Cit - y side-walks, bus-y side-walks dressed in hol-i-day style,
2. Strings of street-lights, ev-en stop-lights blink a bright red and green,

F₇   B♭

In the air there's a feel-ing of Christ-mas. _____
As the shop-pers rush home with their treas-ures. _____

B♭   E♭

Child-ren laugh-ing, peo-ple pass-ing, meet-ing smile af - ter smile,
Hear the snow crunch, see the kids bunch, this is San-ta's big scene,

F₇   B♭

And on ev'-ry street cor - ner you hear: _____
And a-bove all this bus - tle you hear: _____

B REFRAIN

B♭   E♭

Sil - ver bells, _____ (Sil - ver bells,)   Sil - ver bells, _____ (Sil - ver bells,)

It's Christ - mas time in the cit - y. ___

Ring - a - ling, ___ (Ring - a - ling,) Hear them ring, ___ (Hear them ring,)

Soon it will be Christ - mas day. ___

Listen for the jingle of the sleigh bells and the crack of the whip in this lively music.

Sleigh Ride
Leroy Anderson

CD 8-26

A FESTIVAL OF LIGHTS

O Chanukah   CD 9-1, 2

English Words by Judith Eisenstein   *Jewish Folk Song*

O Cha - nu - kah, O cha - nu - kah, come light the me - no - rah.
Let's __ have a par - ty, we'll all dance the ho - rah.

Gath - er round the ta - ble, we'll give you a treat.

Shin - ing tops to play with and pan - cakes to eat;

And while we are play - ing, The can - dles are burn - ing __ low,

One for each night, they __ shed a sweet light to re -

1. mind us of days long a - go,

2. mind us of days long a - go.

From THE GATEWAY TO JEWISH SONG, by Judith Eisenstein. Reprinted by permission of the author.

Follow the music in your book as you listen to the recording of "O Chanukah." Can you tell when the voices are singing in unison? In harmony?

Breaking The PIÑATA

Children in Mexico celebrate Christmas Eve in a special way. Read the words of this song to find out why this is such an exciting time of year.

Piñata Song (Al quebrar la piñata) CD 9-3

English Words by Verne Muñoz   Christmas Song from Mexico

In the hap - py days of Christ - mas, _____
En las no - ches de po - sa - das, _____

Sounds of glad - ness fill the air; _____
La pi - ña - ta es lo me - jor; _____

When it's time for the pi - ña - ta, _____
La ni - ña más re - mil - ga - da _____

There's ex - cite - ment ev - 'ry - where. _____
Se al - bo - ro - ta con ar - dor. _____

1. Take a stick and whack it, Be the one to crack it;
2. *Da - le, da - le, da - le, no pier - das el ti - no,*

Win pi - ña - ta's treas - ure, Can - dies for your pleas - ure.
Que de la dis - tan - cia se pier - de el ca - mi - no.

Percussion Accompaniment for Section B

Maracas

Claves

Carol from Puerto Rico

If you were to spend Christmas in Puerto Rico, you would say Merry Christmas this way: "¡Felices Pascuas!"

Oh, Be Joyful   *(Alegría, alegría, alegría)*

English Words by Aura Kontra   *Carol from Puerto Rico*   **CD 9-4, 5**

REFRAIN

G

Oh,   re - joice   in   the   joy   of   this   morn - ing,

A - le - grí - a; a - le   grí - a; a - le - grí - a,

Oh, re - joice in the joy of this day.
A - le - grí - a; a - le - grí - a y pla - cer,

Gen - tle Ma - ry, _____ filled with won - der _____
Que la Vir - gen _____ va de pa - so _____

As she tra - vels _____ on her way. _____
Con su es - po - so _____ ha - cia Be - lén. _____

VERSE

1. Through the dark - ness, _____ trav' - lers wea - ry _____
1. *Ha - cia Be - lén _____ se en ca - mi - nan, _____*

Start their jour - ney, _____ cold and drea - ry.
Ma - ría con su a - man - te es - po - so,

Toward the sta - ble, _steps are turn-ing, _ To the world-ly, _hope re-turn-ing.
Lle - van-do en su _com-pa - ñí - a _ A to-do un Dios _po - de - ro - so.

2. Joyful praises birds are singing,
   To the blessed, rapture bringing.
   Faithful pilgrims, glorifying;
   Son of Mary, all inspiring. *Refrain*

2. *Los pajarillos del bosque*
   Al ver pasar los esposos,
   Les cantaban melodias
   Con sus trinos armoniosos. Refrain

Going A-Caroling

Here We Come A-Wassailing

Carol from England CD 9-6

In the first section of this song, the carolers go from door to door. What do you think they will do when they sing the refrain?

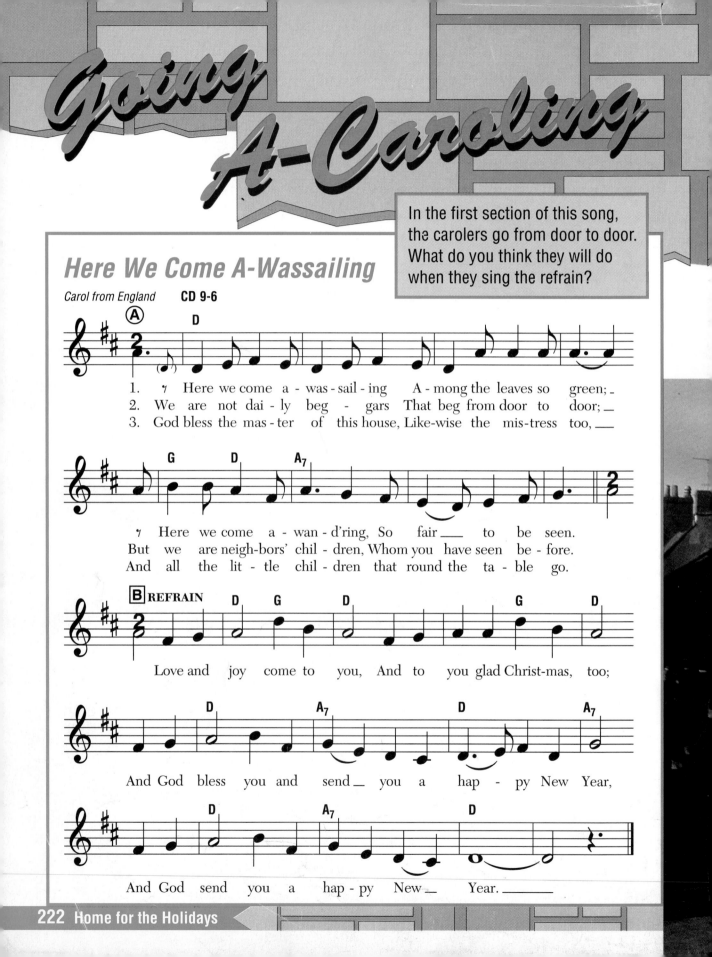

A D
1. 𝄇 Here we come a - was - sail - ing   A - mong the leaves so   green; _
2. We are not dai - ly beg - gars That beg from door to   door; _
3. God bless the mas - ter   of   this house, Like - wise the mis - tress too, __

G   D   A₇
𝄇 Here   we come a - wan - d'ring, So   fair __ to   be   seen.
But   we   are neigh-bors' chil - dren, Whom you   have   seen   be - fore.
And   all   the lit - tle   chil - dren that round the   ta - ble   go.

B REFRAIN   D   G   D   G   D
Love and   joy   come to   you, And   to   you glad Christ-mas,   too;

D   A₇   D   A₇
And God   bless   you and   send __ you   a   hap - py New   Year,

D   A₇   D
And God   send   you   a   hap - py   New __   Year. ____

Added Parts

Descant (Voices or bells)

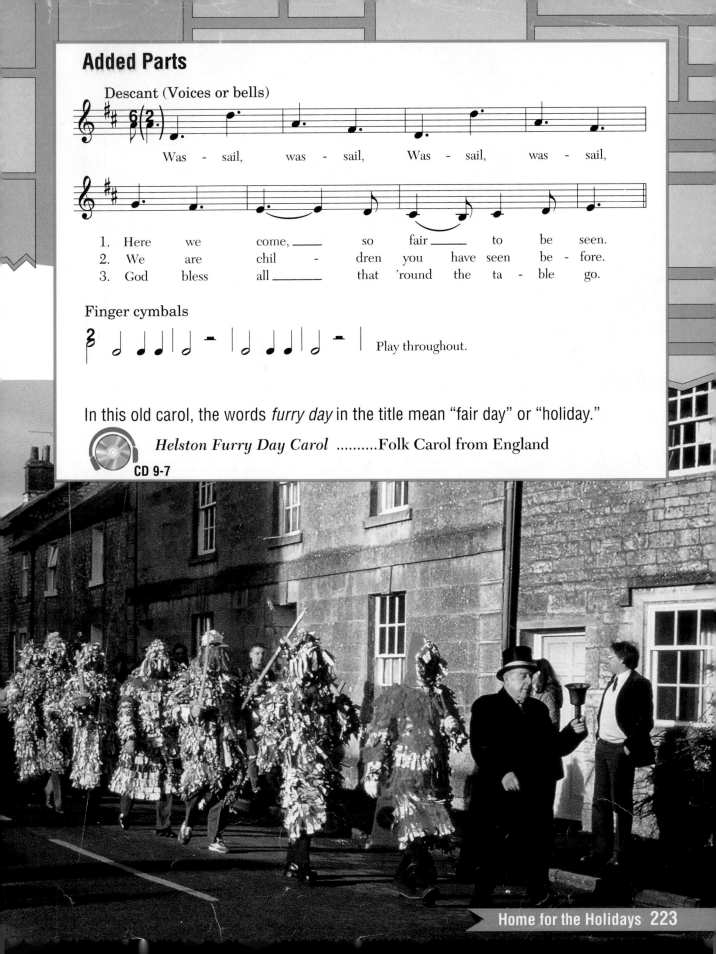

Was - sail,   was - sail,   Was - sail,   was - sail,

1. Here   we   come, _____   so   fair _____   to   be   seen.
2. We   are   chil -   dren   you   have   seen   be - fore.
3. God   bless   all _____   that   'round   the   ta - ble   go.

Finger cymbals

Play throughout.

In this old carol, the words *furry day* in the title mean "fair day" or "holiday."

Helston Furry Day Carol ....Folk Carol from England

CD 9-7

Spanish-speaking people often accompany their carols with percussion instruments. Try playing a tambourine on the words *fum, fum, fum* when they come in the song.

JOIN THE CHORUS

Fum, Fum, Fum   CD 9-8

English Words by Aura Kontra   *Carol from Catalonia*

1. On De-cem-ber five and twen-ty,
2. Come with us and join the cho-rus, fum, fum,
En di-ciem-bre vein-ti-cin-co,

fum.

On De-cem-ber five and twen-ty,
Come with us and join the cho-rus,
En di-ciem-bre vein-ti-cin-co,

fum, fum, fum.

Sing with joy this hap-py
Ha na-ci-do un ni-

morn, Play the drum and sound the horn. On this
ñito, ro-sa-di-to y blan-quito, Hi-jo

day good tid - ings bring - ing, Heav'n and earth to -
de la Vir - gen pu - ra, Que ha na - ci - do en

geth - er sing - ing, fum, fum, fum.
un es - ta - blo,

Bells and Drum

Here are two parts you can play to accompany "Fum, Fum, Fum."

Bells and drum

Three Kings Day

Children in Puerto Rico receive gifts on Three Kings' Day, which is celebrated on the sixth of January.

Three Kings (Los tres Santos Reyes)

CD 9-9

English Words by Aura Kontra   Carol from Puerto Rico

1. Three __ kings are com - ing, __ how ho - ly __ they are,
1. Los tres San - tos Rey - es, __ los tres y __ los tres,

Three __ kings are com - ing, __ how ho - ly __ they are.
Los tres San - tos Rey - es, __ los tres y __ los tres.

In good faith we'll greet them, __ for they've trav - eled far,
Los sa - lu - da - re - mos __ con di - vi - na fe,

In good faith we'll greet them, __ for they've trav - eled far.
Los sa - lu - da - re - mos __ con di - vi - na fe.

2. Carefully they follow a star shining bright, *(2 times)*
   Weary steps move slowly, and cold is the night. *(2 times)*

3. It is time to leave you, we're going away, *(2 times)*
   Happy, happy New Year to all here today. *(2 times)*

2. *Llegan con cautela, la estrella los guia.* (2 times)
   Se sienten sus pasos en la noche fria. (2 times)

3. *Señores, adiós, porque ya nos vamos.* (2 times)
   Todos los presentes pasen feliz año. (2 times)

Accompaniment Patterns

These patterns can be played throughout the song.

Maracas

Guiro

Autoharp strum

Add a Countermelody

You can sing this countermelody. You can also play it on bells or recorder.

Voices, bells, or recorder

La,   la,   la,   la,   la,   la,   la, la, la, la;

La,   la,   la,   la,   la,   la,   la, la, la, la.

A SPECIAL HOLIDAY

The holiday celebration known as Kwanzaa was created to remind African Americans of their heritage.

Harambee

Words and Music by James McBride

1. We gath-er for the Kwan-zaa hol-i-day this time each year_ With
2. Sev-en dif-fer-ent prin-ci-ples that help us learn to grow_ We
3. Build-ing as a na-tion with our hon-or and our pride,_ We

rel-a-tives and friends from far and wide,__
cel-e-brate our faith and u-ni-ty,___
learn to hon-or truth and show our love,__

Shar-ing in a peace-ful time of trust and love and song,_ With
Hop-ing that the best_ of all your wish-es do come true,_ We
Car-ing is a part_ of our re-spon-si-bil-i-ty._ We

joy e-nough to last__ the whole year long.
wish a hap-py Kwan-zaa to you.
want the world to live__ in har-mo-ny.

REFRAIN

Kwan-zaa hol-i-day_ is a spe-cial hol-i-day,_ A
ram-bee__ means_ hel-lo and good-bye, too,_ A

1.
time to cel-e-brate_ our his-to-ry. Ha-

2.
way of show-ing that__ I care for you.

EARTH DAY

A Theme Musical
by Carmino Ravosa

Life Ain't What It Used to Be

CD 9-12, 19

Words by Margaret Jones   Music by Carmino Ravosa

Not so ver-y long a-go, the best things in life were free.

But to-day that all has changed. Life ain't what it used to be.

Life ain't what it used to be,

not the way it used to be,

not the way it used to be then.

East and West and in be-tween, rain was pure and for-ests green.

Words © 1991 Margaret Jones.

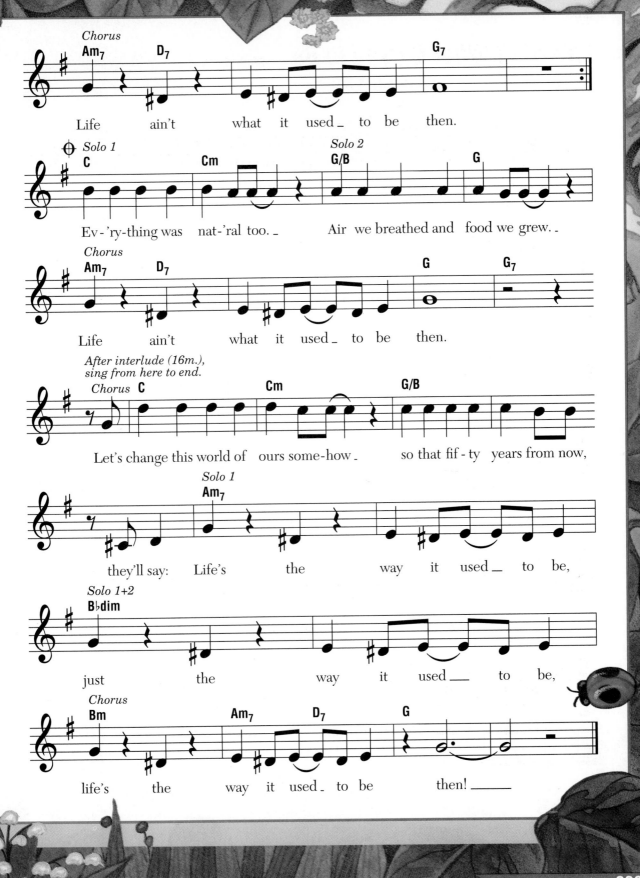

Do What's Right with What's Left

CD 9-13, 21

Words and Music by Carmino Ravosa

Gone Forever

CD 9-14, 23

Words and Music by Carmino Ravosa

When they're gone they're gone for-ev-er, gone for-ev-er,

When they're gone they're gone, _____ gone, _____

gone for-ev-er. When they're gone they're gone for-ev-er,

gone. _____ When they're gone they're gone, _____

gone for-ev-er, gone for-ev-er.

gone, _____ gone. _____

When are we gon-na learn? When are we gon-na see? That

Spoken 2nd verse:
Over 4,000 species of wildlife all over the world
face the threat of extinction. Animals such as the
giant panda, the blue whale, the whooping crane,
and the black rhinoceros will disappear unless more
protective action is taken.   *(Repeat to B)*

Change the Way We Live

CD 9-15, 24

Words and Music by Carmino Ravosa

rit. last time — *Fine*

Change the way we live, we've got to change the way we live.

1. We've got to show that the world is in trou - ble, _____
2. We've got to show __ that each liv - ing crea - ture _____ is

how ev - 'ry - one must care.
u - nique in ev - 'ry way. That

Show that the world is in trou - ble, _____
care - less - ness, greed, and in - diff - 'rence _____

and all peo - ple must do their share. We've got to
must be from some oth - er day.

Make This World a Better Place

CD 9-16, 25

Words and Music by Carmino Ravosa

Let's Make Each Day Earth Day

Words by Margaret Jones   Music by Carmino Ravosa   **CD 9-17, 26**

Solo 1

Let's make each day earth day, to val - ue and hold dear.

Let's give earth a birth - day, each day of the year.

Chorus

(Hap-py earth day!   Hap-py earth day!)   (Hap-py Earth day!   Hap-py Earth day!)

Solo 2

We'll pro - tect our o - ceans, re - new our pre - cious land.

And make each day earth day if we all lend a hand.

Chorus

(Hap-py earthday! Hap-py earthday!) (Hap-py Earthday! Hap-py Earthday!)

And with ev - 'ry can - dle, a prom-ise that will last.

Countermelody

We will make the fu - ture bet - ter than the past.

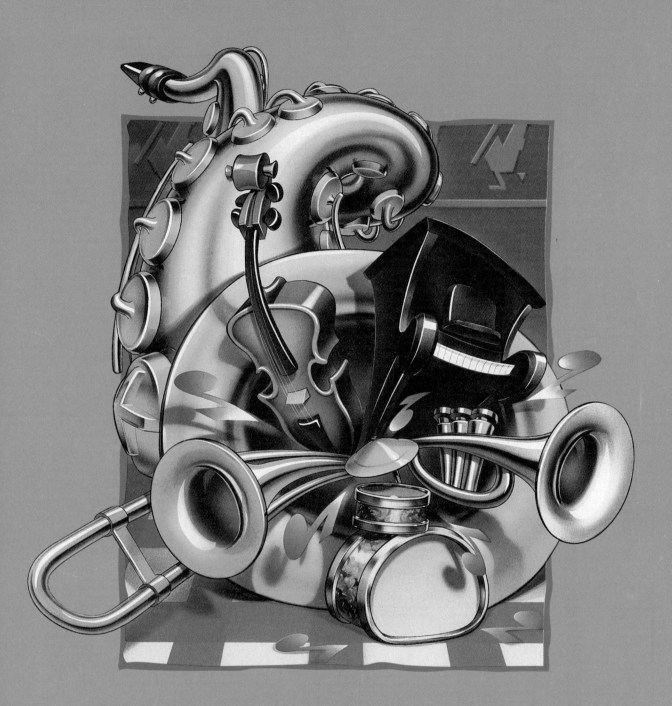

READING

Do you know the score?

You can read the lyrics,
or words of a song.

This section of your book will
help you read the music as well. As you
progress from lesson to lesson in an orderly
fashion, you will learn to translate symbols
into sound. In other words, you'll learn to
interpret-to read-the music score.

So make the "Reading Connection" and
you'll soon know the score!

section

Curious Advice

What advice does Grandma Grundt give the children in the old American folk songs on this page and the next?

Grandma Grundt CD 9-28

Mountain Song from North Carolina

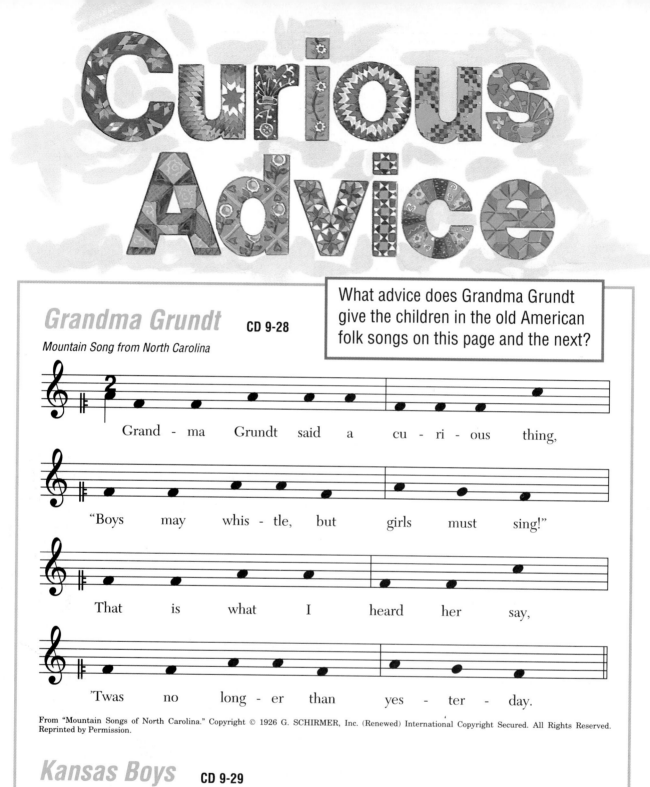

Grand - ma Grundt said a cu - ri - ous thing,

"Boys may whis - tle, but girls must sing!"

That is what I heard her say,

'Twas no long - er than yes - ter - day.

Kansas Boys CD 9-29

Folk Song from the United States

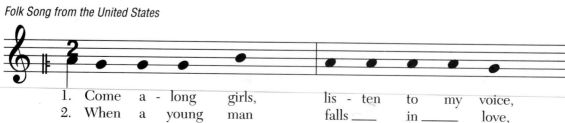

1. Come a - long girls, lis - ten to my voice,
2. When a young man falls ___ in ___ love,

Don't you ev - er mar - ry those good for no - thing boys.
First ___ its ___ "hon - ey" and then "tur - tle ___ dove,"

If you do your fate will be,
Till he hears the fid - dle be play,

Hoe - cake, ho - mi - ny, and sas - sa - fras tea.
On his hap - py ___ wed - ding day.

PENTATONIC SCALES

Each song on pages 244 and 245 uses a different pentatonic scale.

Cotton-Eye Joe   CD 9-30

Folk Song from Tennessee

Where did you come from, where did you go?

Where did you come from, Cot - ton - Eye ___ Joe?

The Death of the Robin CD 9-31

Folk Song from the United States   *Adapted by Jean Sinor*

Who killed the Ro - bin? Who killed the Ro - bin?

"I," said the spar - row, "with my lit - tle bow and ar - row,

It was I, oh it was I."

The Riddle Song CD 9-32

Folk Song from Kentucky

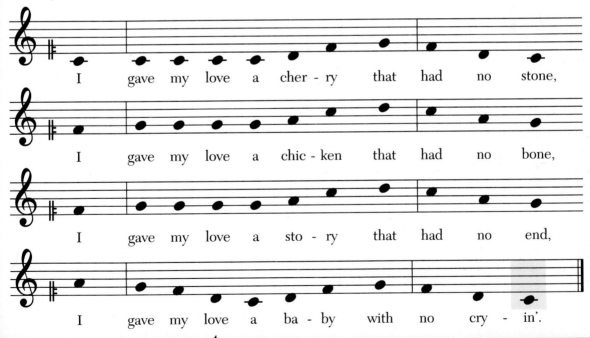

I gave my love a cher - ry that had no stone,

I gave my love a chic - ken that had no bone,

I gave my love a sto - ry that had no end,

I gave my love a ba - by with no cry - in'.

Crawdad Hole

CD 9-33

Folk Song from the United States

1. You get a line and I'll get a pole, Honey,
   You get a line and I'll get a pole, Babe.
   You get a line and I'll get a pole,
        We'll go fishin' in a crawdad hole,
   Honey, Baby mine.

2. Sittin' on a bank till my feet get cold, Honey,
   Sittin' on a bank till my feet get cold, Babe.
   Sittin' on a bank till my feet get cold,
        Lookin' down that crawdad hole,
   Honey, Baby mine.

3. What you gonna do if the pond is dry, Honey?
   What you gonna do if the pond is dry, Babe?
   What you gonna do if the pond is dry?
        Sit on the bank, catch an old horsefly,
   Honey, Baby mine.

This song pokes fun at Michie Banjo for putting on airs.

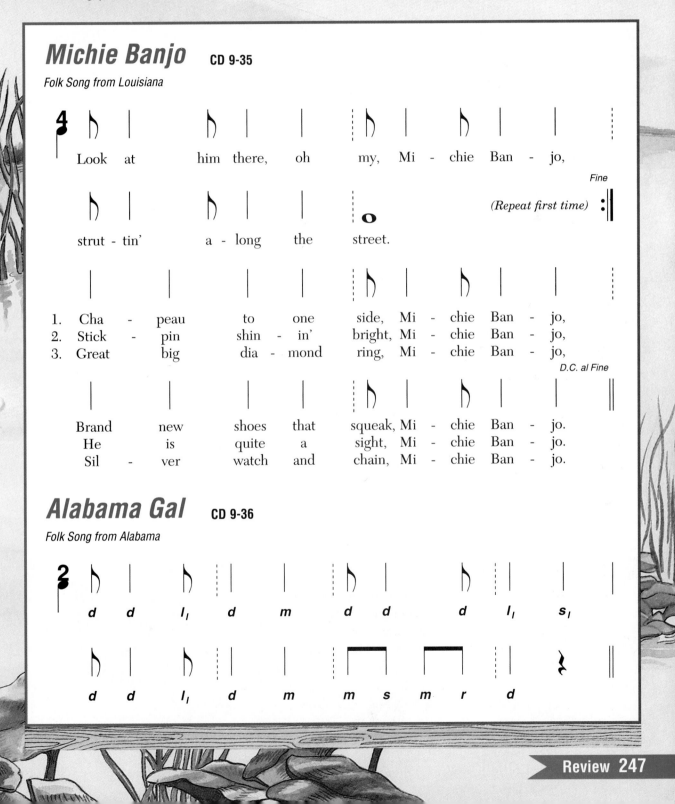

Michie Banjo   CD 9-35

Folk Song from Louisiana

Look at him there, oh my, Mi - chie Ban - jo,

strut - tin' a - long the street.

Fine

(Repeat first time)

1. Cha - peau to one side, Mi - chie Ban - jo,
2. Stick - pin shin - in' bright, Mi - chie Ban - jo,
3. Great big dia - mond ring, Mi - chie Ban - jo,

D.C. al Fine

Brand new shoes that squeak, Mi - chie Ban - jo.
He is quite a sight, Mi - chie Ban - jo.
Sil - ver watch and chain, Mi - chie Ban - jo.

Alabama Gal   CD 9-36

Folk Song from Alabama

d   d   l,   d   m   d   d   d   l,   s,

d   d   l,   d   m   m   s   m   r   d

Can you follow the melody line in this two-part arrangement? The melody starts off on the lower staff, then continues on the upper staff. On which staff does the countermelody start?

Canoe Song CD 9-37

Words and Music by Margaret E. McGhee

Keen and bright, pad - dles sing.

My pad - dle's keen and bright, Flash-ing with sil - ver,

Fol - low the wild goose flight, Dip, dip and swing.

Wild geese fly on the wing.

You can play this drum part to accompany the two-part arrangement of "Canoe Song," on page 248 in your book. Practice the drum part this way.

SAY the rhythm syllables and the *boom-di-di* words. CLAP the part. PLAY the part on an instrument.

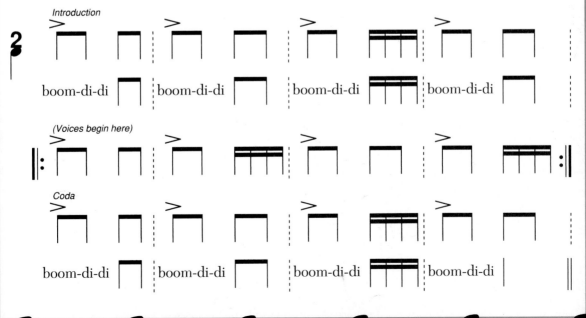

Drum Part

Introduction

boom-di-di   boom-di-di   boom-di-di   boom-di-di

(Voices begin here)

Coda

boom-di-di   boom-di-di   boom-di-di   boom-di-di

AN OLD FAVORITE

Follow the chart as you sing this song.

Crawdad Hole   CD 9-33

Folk Song from the United States

You get a   line and   I'll get a   pole,   Hon-ey. ————————————

You get a   line and   I'll get a   pole,   Babe. ————————————

You get a   line and   I'll get a   pole,   We'll go   fishin' in the   crawdad   hole,

Honey, ——————   Ba - ——— by   mine! ————————————

Follow the notation as you listen to this song.

Chickalileeo CD 9-38

Traditional

1. La - la - la-chick-a - li - lee - o,   La - la - la-chick-a - li - lee - o,

I'm gon-na mar - ry   who   I   please,   La - la - la-chick-a - li - lee - o.

2. I'll bet you I will if you marry me, . . .
   La la la la chickalileeo, . . .

3. Now I'm goin' to marry little Johnny Green, . . .
   He's the prett'est boy I've ever seen, . . .

4. But he's gone off to the war away, . . .
   He'll come back some pretty fair day, . . .

5. Now yonder he comes, I do believe, . . .
   I hope he will marry me, . . .

Song with 2 Voice Parts

Can you find the melody line in this two-part arrangement of "Land of the Silver Birch"? On which staff does the countermelody begin?

Land of the Silver Birch CD 9-39

Folk Song from Canada

From a collection of Edith Fouke.

rock - y shore, I'll re - turn.

Blue lake and rock - y shore, I shall re - turn once more.

Repeat and fade out

Boom-di-di-ah - da   Boom-di-di-ah - da

Boom-di-di-ah - da   Boom-di-di-ah - da

RISE AND SHINE

When you can sing "Solfa Canon," try singing it with the words printed below.

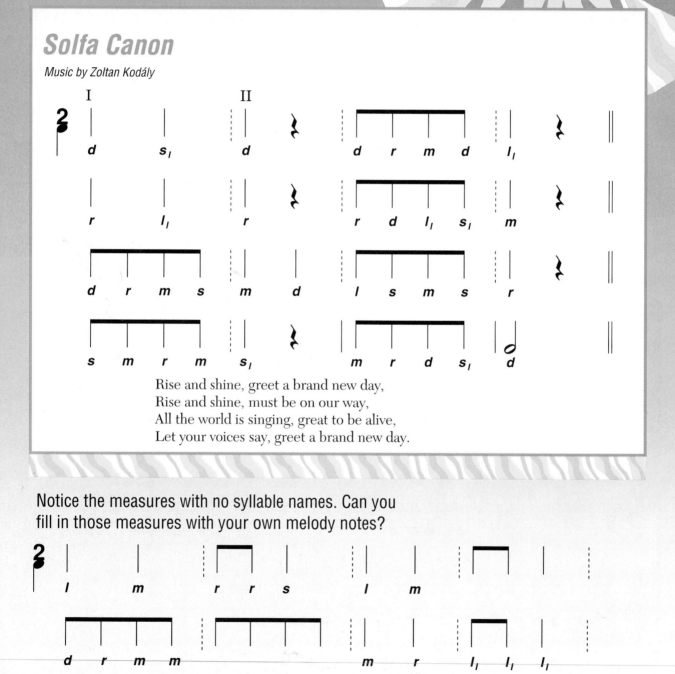

Solfa Canon

Music by Zoltan Kodály

Rise and shine, greet a brand new day,
Rise and shine, must be on our way,
All the world is singing, great to be alive,
Let your voices say, greet a brand new day.

Notice the measures with no syllable names. Can you fill in those measures with your own melody notes?

GATEWAY TO THE WEST

Cumberland Gap was the main gateway for the westbound pioneer settlers. Here are some of the verses the pioneers sang.

Cumberland Gap
CD 9-40

Play-Party Song from Kentucky

1. Lay down boys, take a little nap, . . . (*3 times*)
   Forty-one miles to Cumberland Gap.

Refrain Cumberland Gap, Cumberland Gap . . .
   Ooo, Hoo, Way low down in Cumberland Gap.

2. Cumberland Gap is a mighty fine place, . . .
   Three kinds of water to wash your face.

   Refrain

3. Cumberland Gap with its cliffs and rocks, . . .
   Home of the panther, bear, and fox.

   Refrain

4. Me and my wife and my wife's grandpap, . . .
   We raise cain at Cumberland Gap.

      Refrain

Read the rhythm syllables for "Hey, Betty Martin." Then sing the song with the words.

Hey, Betty Martin   CD 9-41

Folk Song from the United States

Hey, Bet-ty Mar-tin,   Tip-toe, Tip-toe,   Hey, Bet-ty Mar-tin,   Tip-toe, fine;

Hey, Bet-ty Mar-tin,   Tip-toe, Tip-toe,   Hey, Bet-ty Mar-tin,   Tip-toe, fine.

Five Scales—Five Shapes

All pentatonic scales have five tones. Each scale has its own special sound and takes its name from the first note of the scale. Look at the diagrams below. Can you make your fingers show the shape of these pentatonic scales?

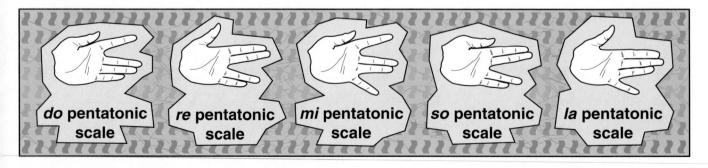

do pentatonic scale   *re* pentatonic scale   *mi* pentatonic scale   *so* pentatonic scale   *la* pentatonic scale

PLAYING PENTATONIC SCALES

Play pentatonic scales on a xylophone.

Weevily Wheat   CD 9-42

Traditional

Don't want your wee - vi - ly wheat, don't want your bar - ley,

Take some flour in half an hour and bake a cake for Char - lie.

Five times five is twen - ty five, Five times six is thir - ty,

Five times sev'n is thir - ty - five, Five times eight is for - ty.

READ A MELODY

Kansas Boys
CD 9-29

Folk Song from the United States

Rhythm Canon

When you can read the rhythm, perform it in canon with a friend.

Music for Two People

Why Shouldn't My Goose?   CD 9-43

Folk Song from England

I   II

Why should-n't my goose grow as fat as thy goose,

When I paid for my goose twice as much as thou?

Sing and Clap

Sing

Clap

An AMERICAN Lullaby

Susan Comforting the Baby   *Mary Cassatt*

Hush, Little Baby   CD 9-44

Folk Song from the United States

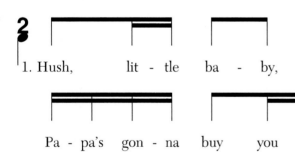

1. Hush, lit - tle ba - by, don't say a word,

Pa - pa's gon - na buy you a mock - ing - bird.

2. If that mockingbird won't sing,
   Papa's gonna buy you a di'mond ring.

3. If that di'mond ring turns to brass,
   Papa's gonna buy you a looking glass.

4. If that looking glass gets broke,
   Papa's gonna buy you a billy goat.

5. If that billy goat won't pull,
   Papa's gonna buy you a cart and bull.

6. If that cart and bull turn over,
   Papa's gonna buy you a dog named Rover.

7. If that dog named Rover won't bark,
   Papa's gonna buy you a horse and cart.

8. If that horse and cart fall down,
   You'll be the sweetest little one in town.

As collected by Jean Ritchie.

BALANCING ACT

When you sing the Spanish words, change the number of elephants each time you sing. Here are the Spanish words for two through ten: *dos, tres, cuatro, cinco, seis, siete, ocho, nueve, diez.*

CD 9-45
An Elephant (Un elefante)

English Words by Alice Firgau Folk Song from Chile

There on a cobweb made by a spider
Sat a big elephant a- swingin'.
Then just to see just how strong it could be, he
Called for a friend to come and join 'im.

*Un elefante se balanceaba
sobre la tela de una araña.
Como veía que resistía,
fue a llamar a un camarada.*

LONELY BIRD

How do you think this song should be sung? Can you think of adjectives that might describe the mood that is suggested by the words?

In the Silent Forest CD 9-46

Words by Jean Sinor   Folk Song from Hungary

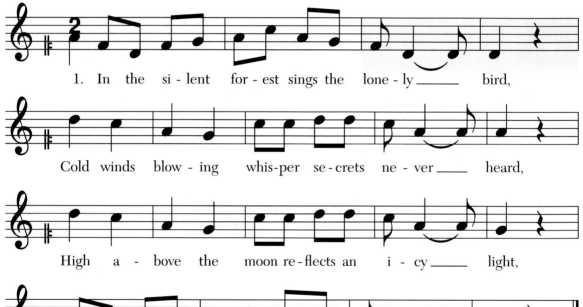

1. In the si - lent for - est sings the lone - ly ____ bird,
Cold winds blow - ing whis-per se - crets ne - ver ____ heard,
High a - bove the moon re - flects an i - cy ____ light,
Sha - dows flee - ing swift - ly through the au - tumn ____ night.

2. Through the misty treetop flies the orphaned lark,
Forest branches creaking stiffly, bare and stark.
Sadly sounds the plaintive calling high above,
Calling in the autumn shadows for his love.

2-Voice Rhythm Piece

This rhythm piece can be performed by two groups, two individuals, or by one person using both hands. Try it all three ways.

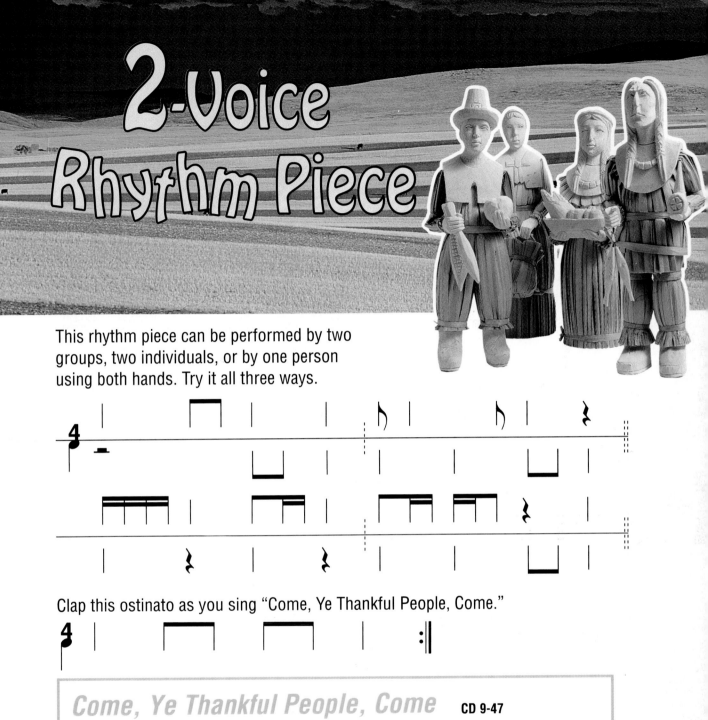

Clap this ostinato as you sing "Come, Ye Thankful People, Come."

Come, Ye Thankful People, Come   CD 9-47

Words by Henry Alford   *Music by George J. Elvey*

1. Come, ye thankful people, come,
   Raise the song of harvest home;
   All is safely gathered in,
   Ere the winter storms begin;
   God, our Maker, doth provide
   For our wants to be supplied;
   Come to God's own temple, come,
   Raise the song of harvest home.

2. All the blessings of the field,
   All the stores the gardens yield;
   All the fruits in full supply,
   Ripened 'neath the summer sky;
   All that spring with bounteous hand
   Scatters o'er the smiling land;
   All the liberal autumn pours
   From her rich o'erflowing stores.

The TUNE DETECTIVE

Can you figure out the name of this song by using the few rhythm and melody clues that are given? When you know what it is, sing the song with the words.

Trace the Contour

The contour, or shape, of a melody gives you a clue to a song's title.

Here is the contour, or shape, of the first few measures of "Chairs to Mend."

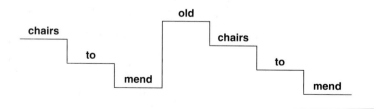

MISSING MELODY PARTS

Notice the places where there are no solfa syllables.

Clap Your Hands   CD 9-49

Folk Song from the United States

d   d   d d r d   s₁ s₁
Clap, clap, clap your hands, Clap your hands to - geth - er,

d   d   m m r r d   d
Clap, clap, clap your hands, Clap your hands to - geth - er.

From AMERICAN FOLK SONGS FOR CHILDREN, collected by Ruth Seeger.

Look at the four contour pictures below. Which picture shows the missing melody part in "Clap Your Hands"?

1.
hands
your
clap

2.
clap
your
hands

3.
your
clap
hands

4.
clap
hands
your

These contour diagrams show parts of three songs you know. Follow the diagrams as you sing each song. Can you hear the notes that are the same in each song?

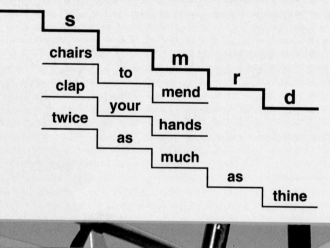

Can You Read This?

Here is a new melody for you to read.

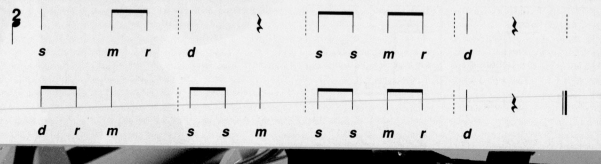

s m r d   s s m r d

d r m   s s m   s s m r d

PIPES & FIDDLES

Song of the Shepherds CD 10-1

English Words by Marion Bergman Carol from Czechoslovakia

1. Shepherds, leave your flocks tonight,
   Follow yonder star so bright.

Refrain Haidom, haidom, tidlidom,
   Haidom, haidom, tidlidom.
   Haidom, haidom, tidlidom,
   Haidom, haidom, tidlidom.

2. Hearken to the angels' words,
   Rise and leave your flocks and herds.

   Refrain

3. In a manger low He lies,
   Praises echo through the skies.

   Refrain

4. Shepherds come you now away,
   On your pipes and fiddles play.

   Refrain

AN OLD FAVORITE

Sing "Clap Your Hands," first with solfa syllables, then with letter names.

Clap Your Hands

Folk Song from the United States   CD 9-49

From AMERICAN FOLK SONGS FOR CHILDREN, collected by Ruth Seeger.

Adding *fa*'s

Turn back to page 266 in your book and sing the melody that is shown at the bottom of the page. Can you put some *fa*'s into the melody? Try adding extra notes, or change some of the notes that are already there.

Canon with *fa*

Here is a canon with *fa*'s written in it. Your class can sing it in unison, then in canon.

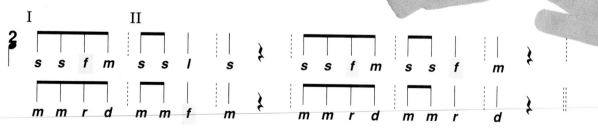

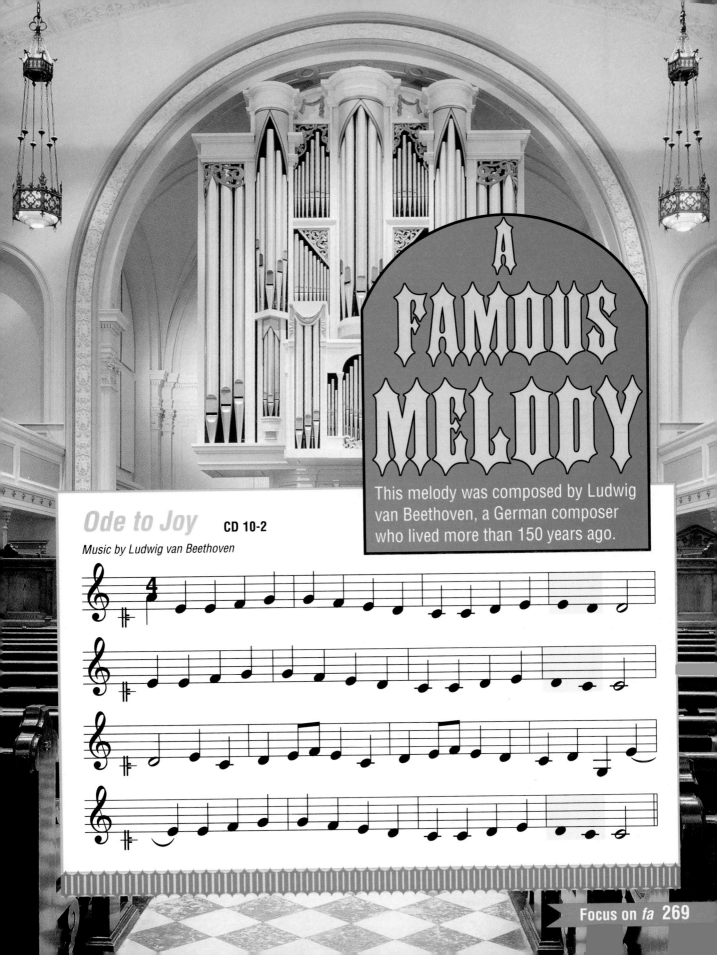

Ode to Joy CD 10-2

Music by Ludwig van Beethoven

A FAMOUS MELODY

This melody was composed by Ludwig van Beethoven, a German composer who lived more than 150 years ago.

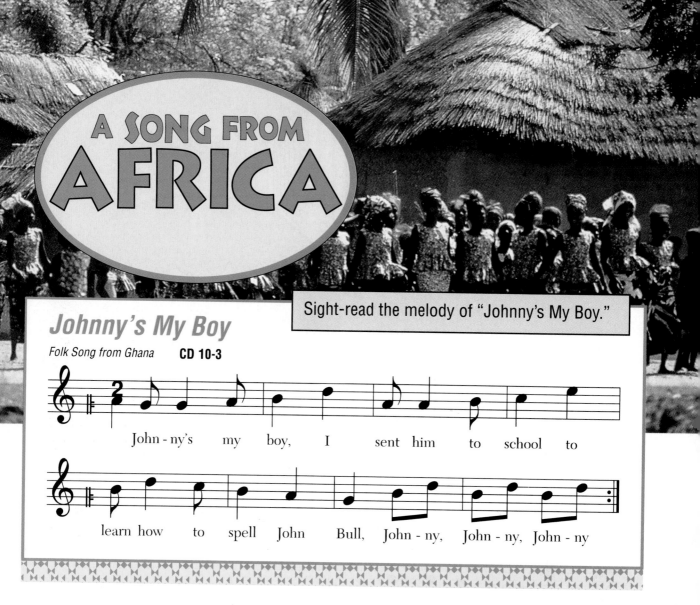

A SONG FROM AFRICA

Johnny's My Boy

Folk Song from Ghana **CD 10-3**

Sight-read the melody of "Johnny's My Boy."

John - ny's my boy, I sent him to school to learn how to spell John Bull, John - ny, John - ny, John - ny

Three Scales

Do pentatonic scale: *d r m s l*

Do pentachordal scale: *d r m f s*

Do hexachordal scale: *d r m f s l*

Which scale is used in this melody?

FOLK SONG FROM CHILE

Notice that this song has many *fa*'s.
Sing it first with solfa syllables, then
with letter names.

San Severino   CD 10-6

Folk Song from Chile

San   Se - ve - ri - no,   la   bue - na, bue - na   vi - da;
sahn   seh - veh - ree - noh lah   bweh - nah bweh - nah vee - dah

San   Se - ve - ri - no,   la   bue - na, bue - na   vi - da.
sahn   seh - veh - ree - noh lah   bweh - nah bweh - nah vee - dah

Name the Scale

What pitches are used in this melody? Can you name the scale of this
familiar canon?

Dance Song From Czechoslovakia

Three Different *do*'s

Here is the beginning of a song called "Dancing." The music is notated using three different *do*'s.

The Birch Tree   CD 10-9

Folk Song from Russia

1. See the lovely birch in the meadow,
   Curly leaves all dancing when the wind blows.
   Loo-lee-loo, when the wind blows. *(2 times)*

2. Oh, my little tree, I need branches,
   For three silver flutes I need three branches,
   Loo-lee-loo, three branches. *(2 times)*

3. From another branch I will make now,
   I will make a tingling balalaika,
   Loo-lee-loo, balalaika. *(2 times)*

4. When I play my new balalaika,
   I will think of you, my lovely birch tree,
   Loo-lee-loo, lovely birch tree. *(2 times)*

Recorder Countermelody

CD 9-44

Here is an arrangement of "Hush, Little Baby" for voices and recorder.

Hush, Little Baby

Folk Song from the United States   *Collected by Jean Ritchie*

Hush, lit-tle ba-by, don't say a word,   Pa-pa's gon-na buy you a mock-ing bird.

If that mock-ing bird don't sing,   Pa-pa's gon-na buy you a di'-mond ring.

Make up a melody to go with this rhythm. Use at least one *fa* in your melody.

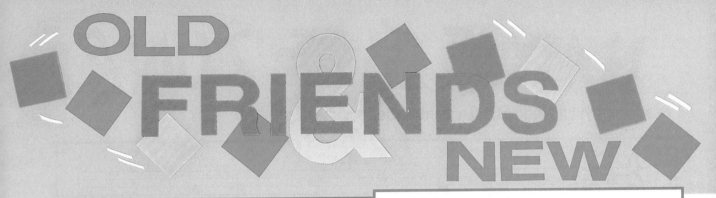

OLD FRIENDS & NEW

Make New Friends CD 10-10

Can you find the new rhythm pattern in this two-part round about friends?

Round

I

Make new friends, but keep the old,

II

One is sil - ver and the oth - er gold.

Follow the words as you listen to "Charlottetown."

Charlottetown CD 10-11

Folk Song from Southern United States

Charlottetown's burning down, Goodbye, goodbye,
Burning down to the ground. Goodbye, Liza Brown.

Ain't you mighty sorry? Goodbye, goodbye,
Ain't you mighty sorry? Goodbye, Liza Brown.

NAME THE TUNE

Read the rhythm syllables, then identify the song.

Crab Canon

This canon can move backwards! Read the canon forward,
then backward. Two groups can perform it together—one
starting at the beginning,
the other starting at the end.

Using rhythm syllables, read the rhythm of "Somebody's Knockin' at Your Door."

Somebody's Knockin' at Your Door

African American Spiritual   **CD 10-13**

Some - bod - y's knock - in' at your door,

Some - bod - y's knock - in' at your door.

Oh, _____ sin - ner, why don't you ans - wer?

Some - bod - y's knock - in' at your door.

"Goodbye" RHYTHMS

Can you find the rhythms that sound like "goodbye"?

| Charlotte- | town's | burning | down | goodbye ——— ___ | goodbye ——— ___ |

| In the | silent | forest | sings the | lone-ly ——— ___ | bird ———— |

Listen to hear where the "goodbye" rhythm comes in this song.

All Night, All Day   CD 10-14

African American Spiritual

All   night,   all _____ day,

An – gels   watch - ing   o - ver   me,   my ___ Lord. ___

All   night,   all _____ day,

An – gels   watch - ing   o - ver   me.

A Singing Valentine

Honey, You Can't Love One

Folk Song from the United States   **CD 10-15**

1. Hon - ey, you can't love one,
Hon - ey, you can't love one,
You can't love one and still have your fun,
Oh, hon - ey, you can't love one.

2. Honey, you can't love two,   *(2 times)*
You can't love two and always be true,
Oh, honey, you can't love two.

3. Honey, you can't love three,   *(2 times)*
You can't love three and be true to me,
Oh, honey, you can't love three.

SHINE, SHINE, SHINE!

Read the rhythm syllables of "Mister Rabbit." Be extra careful with the rhythm pattern shown in red.

Mister Rabbit

African American Play Song **CD 10-16**

s₁ s₁ d d d d d d r m d r d
1. "Mis - ter Rab - bit, Mis - ter Rab - bit, your ear's might - y long!"

s m m s l s m s
"Yes, my Lord, they're put on wrong," —

s l s m d r m r m s
Ev - 'ry lit - tle soul must shine, shine, shine, —

s l s m d r m d r d
Ev - 'ry lit - tle soul must shine, — shine, shine.

2. "Mister Rabbit, Mister rabbit, your foot's mighty red!"
   "Yes, my Lord, I'm almost dead." *Refrain*

3. "Mister Rabbit, Mister Rabbit, your tail's mighty white!"
   "Yes, my Lord, I'm gettin' outta sight." *Refrain*

THE STORY SONG

A song that tells a story is called a *ballad*. As you listen to the ballad "Streets of Laredo," follow the words below.

Streets of Laredo
CD 10-17

Cowboy Song from the United States

1. As I walked out in the streets of Laredo,
As I walked out in Laredo one day,
I spied a young cowboy wrapped up in white linen,
Wrapped up in white linen and cold as the clay.

2. "I see by your outfit that you are a cowboy,"
These words he said as I boldly walked by.
"Come listen to me and I'll tell my sad story,
I'm shot in the chest and I'm sure I will die."

3. "Now once in the saddle I used to ride handsome,
'A handsome young cowboy' is what they would say,
I'd ride into town and go down to the card-house,
But I'm shot in the chest and I'm dying today."

4. "Go run to the spring for a cup of cold water
To cool down my fever," the young cowboy said.
But when I returned, his poor soul had departed,
And I wept when I saw the young cowboy was dead.

5. We'll bang the drum slowly and play the fife lowly,
We'll play the dead march as we bear him along,
We'll go to the graveyard and lay the sod o'er him;
He was a young cowboy, but he had done wrong.

SONG OF THE BELL TOWER

Lovely Evening
CD 10-18

Traditional Round

I

Oh,   how   love - ly   is   the   eve - ning,   is   the   eve - ning,

II

When   the   bells   are   sweet - ly   ring - ing,   sweet - ly   ring - ing,

III

Ding,   dong,   ding,   dong,   ding,   dong!

Look at the music of "Lovely Evening." What is missing from the notation?

Add an Ostinato

Here is an ostinato to play as an accompaniment for "Lovely Evening."

Finger cymbals

Low F on bass metallophone

The Ringer

Here is a song about a bellringer who wakes everyone too early in the morning.

The Bellringer
CD 10-20

English Words by Jean Sinor   *Folk Song from France*

d	d	d m r	d s,	d
Ev-	'ry	morn- ing at	break of	day,

m	m	m s f	m d	m
That	old	bell- ring- er	starts to	play.

s s s s	s l s	f s f	m
I would like to	sleep, but I	can't ver- y	long,

m m m m	m f m	r s	d
He keeps me a-	wake with his	morn- ing	song.

Wake up! Wake up! Wake up! Wake up! Wake up!

Two Bell Ostinatos

After you have sung "The Bellringer" and "Lovely Evening," on page 282, decide which bell ostinato fits best with each song.

1. Ding - ding - dong, | ding - ding - dong   :||

2. Ding - dong, | ding - dong   :||

Ringing Changes

Many churches in England have a peal of bells in their bell tower. *Ringing changes* means playing the different combinations possible on a given set of bells.

One famous set of four bells is usually played like this.

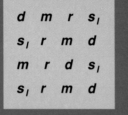

Can you figure out any other changes that can be played on these bells?

The words of an old English folk song tell about many of the famous bells in England.

Oranges and Lemons   CD 10-21

Traditional Song from England

1. "Oranges and lemons," say the bells of St. Clement's;
    "You owe me five farthings," say the bells of St. Martin's;
    "When will you pay me?" say the bells of Old Bailey;
    "When I grow rich," say the bells of Shoreditch;
    "When will that be?" say the bells of Stepney;
    "I do not know," says the great bell of Bow.

2. "Pancakes and fritters," say the bells of St. Peter's;
    "Two sticks and an apple," say the bells of Whitechapel;
    "Old Father Baldpate," say the slow bells of Aldgate;
    "Poker and tongs," say the bells of St. John's;
    "Kettles and pans," say the bells of St. Ann's;
    "Brickbats and tiles," say the bells of St. Giles.

KEEP THE BEAT

Keep the beat as you sing "Love Is Like a Ring."

Love Is Like a Ring   CD 10-22

Traditional Round from Germany

I   II   III   IV

Love is like a ring.___ A ring has__ no end - ing.

When you know this song, make up new verses of your own.

This Old Hammer   CD 10-23

African American Work Song

This old ham - mer, Shines like sil - ver,

Shines like gold, boys, Shines like gold.

In most songs you sing, some beats are stronger and some are weaker. As you sing the songs on this page again, decide which of these beat pictures fits each song.

Strong Beat-Weak Beat

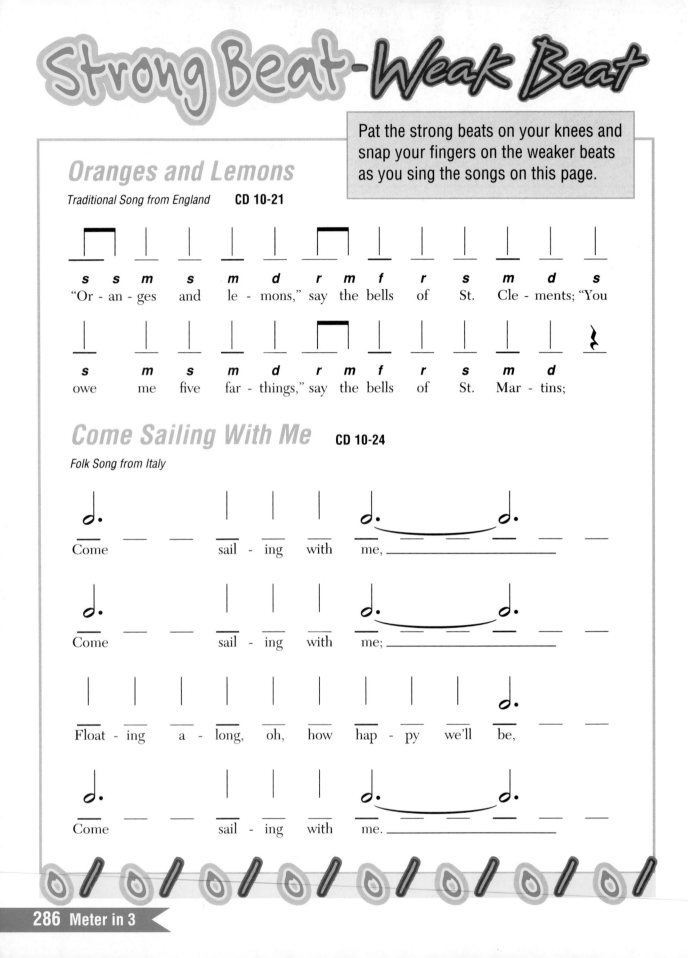

Pat the strong beats on your knees and snap your fingers on the weaker beats as you sing the songs on this page.

Oranges and Lemons

Traditional Song from England   CD 10-21

s s m s m d r m f r s m d s
"Or - an - ges and le - mons," say the bells of St. Cle - ments; "You

s m s m d r m f r s m d
owe me five far - things," say the bells of St. Mar - tins;

Come Sailing With Me   CD 10-24

Folk Song from Italy

Come   sail - ing with me, _____

Come   sail - ing with me; _____

Float - ing a - long, oh, how hap - py we'll be,

Come   sail - ing with me. _____

Conducting the Meter

Notice the meter signature and the bar lines as you sing "Lovely Evening."

Lovely Evening CD 10-18

Traditional Round

I

Oh, how love - ly is the eve - ning, is the eve - ning,

II

When the bells are sweet - ly ring - ing, sweet - ly ring - ing,

III

Ding, dong, ding, dong, ding, dong!

Feel the Meter

As you sing each song listed below, decide whether it moves in a meter of 2 (duple meter) or in a meter of 3 (triple meter). Conducting each song will help you decide.

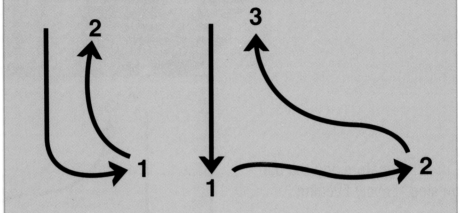

2
1

3
1
2

The Bellringer

Streets of Laredo

The Birch Tree

This Old Hammer

SONG IN TWO METERS

Can you read this song? The following plan will help you to take the challenge.

Pat the strong beats (always the first beat in the measure) and *snap* on the weak beats.

Conduct the meter, beginning with a measure of meter in 3, then a measure of meter in 2, and so forth to the end.

Say the rhythm syllables for the song.

Sing the song with solfa syllables.

Sing the song with words.

The Swallow   CD 10-25

African American Game Song

Lit - tle swal - low, fly to your nest,

Who goes there, fly a fly a - way now.

Lit - tle swal - low, fly to your nest,

Fly a fly a - way

Mountaineer Dance

CD 10-26

The music for this Polish folk dance has two different sections —A and B. Section A is in triple meter; Section B is in duple meter.

The photograph at the top of the page shows the starting position for the dance. Notice that the dancers are standing in groups of three.

Music: Section A

Dance: Step 1

Moving forward, step right, swing, hop; step left, swing, hop. Right, swing, hop; left, swing, hop.

Continue forward.

Repeat Step 1, moving backward.

Music: Section B   Dance: Step 2

Run forward six beats, stamp in place X X X.

Run backward six beats, stamp in place X X X.

Repeat forward and backward.

Music: Section B   Dance: Step 3

Boy (center) and Girl (left) raise arms to form an arch. Girl (right) runs through the arch, followed by Boy. All stamp in place X X X.

Repeat Step 3 with Girl (right) running through the arch. All stamp in place X X X.

Repeat Step 3.

With your classmates, practice Steps 1, 2, and 3. Then do the entire dance with the music, using the following routine.

Section A: Step 1, forward and backward

Section B: Step 2, forward and backward

Section A: Step 1, forward and backward

Section B: Step 3 with repeat

Section A: Step 1, forward and backward

ON THE TRAIL

"Streets of Laredo," the song on page 281 in your book, is a *ballad*—it tells a story. As you listen to "My Home's in Montana," follow the words. Is this song a ballad? Why, or why not?

My Home's in Montana CD 10-27

Words Adapted by W. S. Williams   Cowboy Song from the United States

1. My home's in Montana, I left Indiana
   To start a new life far away in the West;
   My skin's rough as leather, made tough by the weather,
   The wind and the sun of the land I love best.

2. I learned how to lasso way down in El Paso,
   I've followed the cattle wherever they roam;
   I'm weary of strayin', right here I'll be stayin',
   I'll wander no more for Montana's my home.

3. My home's in Montana, I wear a bandana,
   My spurs are of silver, my pony is gray.
   While riding the ranges, my luck never changes,
   With foot in my stirrup I gallop for aye.

4. When valleys are dusty, my pony is trusty,
   He lopes through the blizzards, the snow in his ears.
   The cattle may scatter, but what does it matter?
   My rope is a halter for pig-headed steers.

5. When far from the ranches, I chop the pine branches
   To heap on my campfire as daylight grows pale.
   When I have partaken of beans and of bacon,
   I'll whistle a merry old song of the trail.

Singing Style

As you listen to "White Coral Bells," think of an adjective that describes the performance.

When your class can sing "White Coral Bells" in unison, try singing the song as a two-part round.

White Coral Bells CD 10-28

Round from England

I

White cor - al bells, Up - on a slen - der stalk,
Oh, don't you wish, that you could hear them ring?

II

Lil - ies of the val - ley deck my gar - den walk.
That will hap - pen on - ly when the an - gels sing.

Circle Dance

Yibane Amenu

Round from Israel   **CD 10-29**

The Hebrew words of this song from Israel say, "In our land we shall rebuild our nation." Follow the circle dance below as you listen to the music.

Words:	Yi - ba - ne a - me - nu	b - 'ar - tse ‿ nu;
Steps:	Left stamp Right slide Left step Right slide	Left step Right slide Left step Right slide
Beats:	1 2 3 4	1 2 3 4

(Repeat, moving to the right.)

Words:	B - 'ar - tse - nu	yi - ba - ne
Steps:	Left stamp Right step in Left step in Right step in	Left step in Right step in Left step in Right step in
Beats:	1 2 3 4	1 2 3 4

(Repeat, backing out of the circle.)

Words:	Yi - ba - ne,	Yi - ba - ne.
Steps:	Left step in Right step in Left step in Right stamp	Left step out Right step out Left step in Right step out
Beats:	1 2 3 4	1 2 3 4

Read a Tune

Tap the beat as you listen to "Who Built the Ark?" What can you tell about the rhythm in the color box?

Who Built the Ark?   CD 10-30

African American Spiritual

Who built the ark? No - ah! No - ah!

Who built the ark? Broth - er No - ah built the ark!

Can you read this song without words? Read the rhythm syllables to yourself, then add the solfa syllables.

Song Without Words

Music by Harry R. Wilson

Follow the rhythm notation as you sing the words of this song. Then sing the rhythm syllables from the notation.

Chumbara   CD 10-31

Folk Song from Canada

Chum-ba-ra,   chum-ba-ra, Chum - ba - ra,   chum - ba - ra,

Chum-ba-ra,   chum-ba-ra, Chum, chum, chum, chum, chum, chum, chum, chum,

Chum-ba-ra,   chum-ba-ra, Chum - ba - ra,   chum - ba - ra,

Chum-ba-ra,   chum-ba-ra, chum   chum.

2. Fy-do-lee, . . .   3. Chow-ber-ski, . . .

Clap this ostinato as the class sings "This Old Hammer." Watch the rests!

ROUND AND ROUND

This is really a round round! Show the strong and weak beats as you sing the song. Each strong beat is shown with an accent mark. Notice where the strong beat falls in each phrase.

CD 10-32

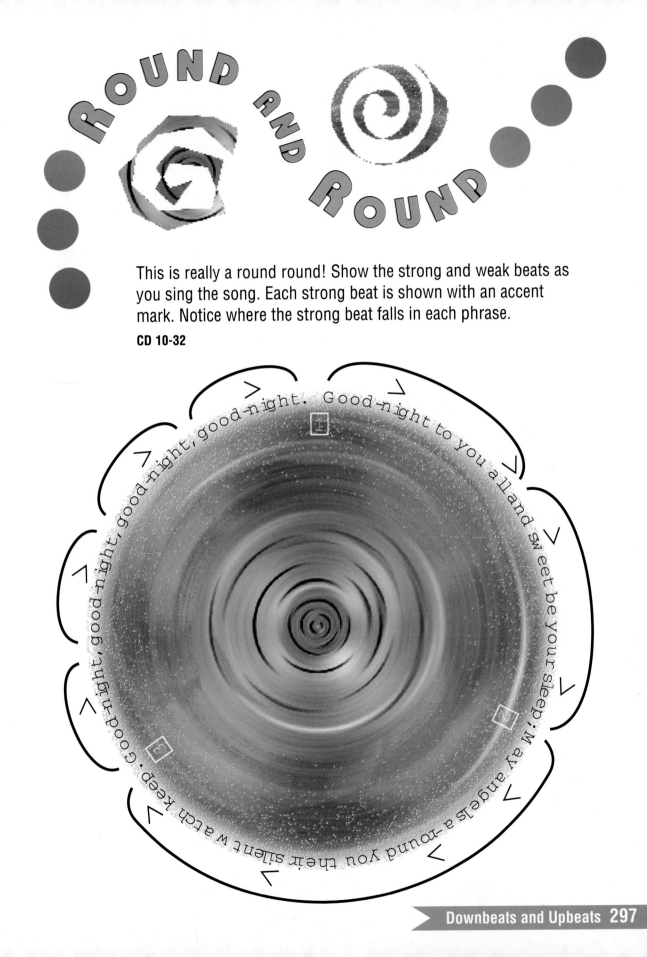

Good-night, good-night. Good-night to you a-ll and sweet be your sleep. May angels a-round you their silent watch keep. Good-night, good-night, good-night, good-night.

DOWNBEATS AND UPBEATS

Shalom Chaverim

Round from Israel **CD 10-33**

Notice the curved lines and the accent marks in "Shalom Chaverim." What do they tell you?

Sha - lom, Cha - ver - im; Sha - lom, cha - ver - im; Sha -

lom, sha - lom; Le -

hit - ra - ot, le - hit - ra - ot, sha -

lom, sha - lom.

Oranges and Lemons

Traditional Song from England **CD 10-21**

Look at the notation. Why are some of the notes in color boxes?

"Or - an - ges and le - mons," say the bells of St. Cle - ment's; "You

owe me five far - things," say the bells of St. Mar - tin's;

UPBEATS and PHRASES

Look at the notation of "Oranges and Lemons" below. Then look at the notation of the same song on page 298 in your book. Are they written the same way? How are they different?

"Or - an - ges and le - mons,"

Say the bells of St. Cle - ment's;

"You owe me five far - things,"

Say the bells of St. Mar - tin's;

Name the Song

Do you know this song? Name the key and the beginning note. Then sing the line with solfa syllables.

Do you remember how a crab canon works? You might want to look back to page 276 in your book.

Here's another crab canon to clap and tap. Read it with rhythm syllables, first forward and then backward.

An Old Favorite

Here is a song you have sung before. Follow the notation as you sing it with your classmates.

The Riddle Song   CD 9-32

Folk Song from Kentucky

I gave my love a cher - ry that had no stone

I gave my love a chic - ken that had no bone,

I gave my love a sto - ry that had no end

I gave my love a ba - by with no cry - in'.

2. How can there be a cherry that has no stone?
   How can there be a chicken that has no bone?
   How can there be a story that has no end?
   How can there be a baby with no cryin'?

3. A cherry when it's blooming, it has no stone.
   A chicken when its pipping, it has no bone.
   A story that's I love you, it has no end.
   A baby when it's sleeping, has no cryin'.

Early American Song

"Amazing Grace" has been sung and played by many people since the early days of America. Follow the notation as you listen to the song.

Amazing Grace

Words by John Newton Early American Melody CD 10-36

1. A - maz - ing __ grace, how sweet the sound, That
2. 'Twas grace that __ taught my heart to fear, And

saved a _____ wretch like me! _____ I
grace my ___ fears re - lieved; _____ How

once ___ was __ lost, but now ___ am ___ found, Was
pre - cious _ did that grace ___ ap - pear The

blind, but ___ now I see. _____
hour I _____ first be - lieved! _____

3. Through many dangers, toils, and snares,
   I have already come;
   'Tis grace has brought me safe thus far.
   And grace will lead me home.

4. The Lord has promised good to me,
   His word my hope secures;
   He will my shield and portion be,
   As long as life endures.

Add a Countermelody

Here is a countermelody to sing with the melody of "Amazing Grace." When the melody and countermelody are sung together, you will be singing in harmony.

A - maz - ing grace, sweet sound

That __ once saved me, _____

I __ then was lost, now found,

Was __ blind, but now see. _____

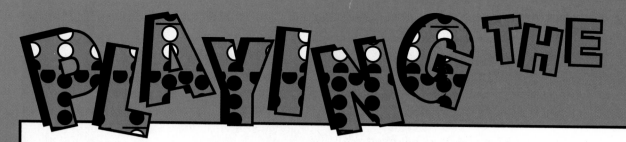

Using the left hand, cover the holes shown in the first diagram.

Cover the top of the mouthpiece with your lips. Blow gently as you whisper *dahh*. You will be playing G.

1. When you can play G, A, and B, you will be able to play the beginning of "Kansas Boys."

2. Practice playing two new notes.

Use them in this countermelody for "Clementine."

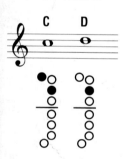

3. Here are more new notes to try. Cover the holes securely with your fingers flat, not arched, and whisper the *dahh*.

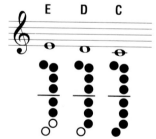

4. Discover how to play F#. You will need it for the melody of "Johnny's My Boy."

5. Learn how to play F on your recorder. Remember to cover the holes securely.

Play F in this ostinato to accompany the round "Goodnight."

6. Add a recorder part to "Mountaineer's Dance." The A section will use notes you know. The B section adds a new note.

SOUND BANK

ARPA (AR pah) A folk harp that has 34-36 nylon strings and spans almost five octaves. It is a diatonic instrument and must be retuned to play in a different key. The arpa is used especially for the *jarocho* music of Veracruz. It is also used in central Mexico, Venezuela, the mountains of Ecuador and Peru, Paraguay, and northern Argentina. (p. 183) **CD 10-46**

BANGDI (BAHNG dee) A short flute made of bamboo. The pipe is closed with a cork at the blowing end and open at the lower end. A blow-hole is located near the cork and six finger-holes are distributed in the middle of the pipe. Today, the bangdi is an important solo and concert instrument in China. (p. 185) **CD 10-38**

BASSOON A large tube-shaped wooden wind instrument with a double reed. Lower notes on the bassoon can be gruff or comical. Higher notes are softer, sweeter, and more gentle-sounding. (p. 125) **CD 10-39**

CELLO A large wooden string instrument. The player sits with the cello between his or her knees and reaches around the front to play it. The cello has a low, rich-sounding voice which can also go up to notes children sing. (p. 124) **CD 10-40**

CLARINET A wind instrument shaped like a long cylinder. It is usually made of wood and has a reed in the mouthpiece. Low notes on the clarinet are soft and hollow. The middle notes are open and bright, and the highest notes are thin and piercing. (p. 125) **CD 10-41**

DUNDUN DRUMS (doon doon) Most of these double-headed drums have an hourglass shape with the ends covered with goatskin drumheads that are fastened together with cords stretched down the length of the drum. Pressing the cords tightens the drumheads, producing sharp, high sounds. Relaxing the pressure on the cords lowers the pitch of the sound produced. (p. 179) **CD 10-42**

FLUTE A small metal instrument shaped like a pipe. The player holds the flute sideways and blows across an open mouthpiece. The flute's voice is pure, clear, and sweet. Its low notes are the same ones children sing, but it can also go very high. (p. 125)   **CD 10-43**

FRENCH HORN A medium-size instrument made of coiled brass tubing. At one end is a large "bell." The player holds the horn on his or her lap and keeps one hand inside the bell. The sound of the horn is very mellow. It can go higher and lower than children's voices, but its best notes are the same ones children sing best. (p. 126)   **CD 10-45**

JARANA (hah RAH nah) An eight-string guitar used to strum rhythmic accompaniments in various *son* ("folk music") ensembles in Mexico. It is used especially in the central Gulf Coast area in playing *jarocho* (pertaining to Veracruz) music. (p. 183) **CD 10-46**

KOTO (KOH toh) A 7- to 17-string zither with movable frets. It is known as the national instrument of Japan. The player sits on the floor, either cross-legged or in a kneeling position. Sound is produced when the player plucks the silk strings, using the fingers and thumb of the right hand, with a bamboo, bone, or ivory plectrum. The sound is similar to that of a harp. (p. 187)   **CD 10-47**

NATIVE AMERICAN FLUTE A handcrafted wind instrument made from wood, cane, clay, bone, or hollowed-out stalk of a plant. The sound of a Native American flute is similar to that of a recorder. Traditionally a solo instrument used for courtship, healing, and ceremonial gatherings, it has become popular in ensemble performances. (p. 88) **CD 10-44**

OBOE   A slender wooden wind instrument with a double reed. In its low voice the oboe can sound mysterious and "oriental." These are the notes children sing. When it goes higher, the sound is thin and sweet. (p. 125)   **CD 10-48**

OUD   (ood) A wooden string instrument with a round back and a flat front. It consists of a large soundbox connected to a short neck. It is played by plucking the strings. (p. 180)   **CD 10-49**

REQUINTO   (reh KEEN toh) A small guitar that is used to play fast melodies. The strings are plucked with a long, thin plastic pick. Like the jarana, the requinto is used in playing *jarocho* songs. (p. 183)   **CD 10-46**

SITAR   (sih TAR) The sitar has seven strings over movable metal frets. Melodies are played on these seven strings. Additional strings beneath the melody strings sound the drone required of all Indian classical music. These additional strings are not plucked, but resonate by sympathetic vibration when the melody strings are plucked. The sound chamber is made of a gourd. (p. 191)   **CD 10-50**

STRING BASS   The largest string instrument, the one with the lowest voice. A string bass is usually taller than a person. The player must stand or sit on a high stool. The string bass has a deep, dark voice. Sometimes it is gruff, sometimes mellow. (p. 124)   **CD 10-51**

TABLA   (TAB lah) A percussion instrument consisting of a pair of small hand-played drums. A variety of sounds—high, low, loud, pitched, unpitched—can be produced by striking in different ways and on different parts of the head. (p. 191)   **CD 10-50**

TIMPANI Large pot-shaped drums, also called "Kettledrums." Unlike most drums, they can be tuned to notes of the scale. The player can use several drums and play a tune. The timpani can sound like a heartbeat or a roll of thunder. Its voice can be a loud "boom," a quiet "thump," or a distant rumble, depending on how it is played. (p. 129)
CD 10-52

TROMBONE A large brass instrument with the loudest voice in the orchestra. It has tubing, a "bell," and a long, curved "slide." The trombone can be loud and brilliant, but its soft voice is mellow. It can play the notes children sing, but also go much lower. (p. 126)
CD 10-53

TRUMPET The smallest brass instrument, but one with a big sound. The trumpet's voice can be loud and bright, but can also sound warm and sweet. Most of its notes are the same as children sing. (p. 126) **CD 10-54**

TUBA The largest brass instrument, the one with the lowest voice. The tuba's low notes are deep and "dark" sounding. The higher ones are hearty and warm. (p. 126) **CD 10-55**

VIOLA A wooden string instrument played like a violin. The viola's voice is similar to the violin's, but deeper, richer, and "darker." (p. 124) **CD 10-56**

VIOLIN A wooden string instrument held under the player's chin. The violin has many different voices. It plays the notes children sing, but can also go much higher. A good player can create many unusual and interesting sounds on the violin. (p. 124)
CD 10-57

GLOSSARY

AB form (p. 70)   A musical plan that has two different parts, or sections.

ABA form (p. 72)   A musical plan that has three sections. The first and last sections are the same. The middle section is different.

accompaniment (p. 115)   Music that supports the sound of the featured performer(s).

ballad (p. 281)   In music, a song that tells a story.

band (p. 130)   A balanced group of instruments consisting of woodwinds, brass, and percussion.

beat (p. 6)   A repeating pulse that can be felt in some music.

brass (p. 126)   A group of wind instruments, including trumpets, French horns, trombones, and tubas, used in bands and orchestras.

chorus (p. 104)   A large group of singers.

coda (p. 95)   A "tail" or short section added at the end of a piece of music.

composer (p. 30)   A person who makes up pieces of music by putting sounds together in his or her own way.

contour (p. 60)   The "shape" of a melody, made by the way it moves upward and downward in steps and leaps, and by repeated tones.

countermelody (p. 116)   A melody that is played or sung at the same time as another melody.

duet (p. 104)   A composition written for two performers.

dynamics (p. 66)   The loudness and softness of sound.

form (p. 70)   The overall plan of a piece of music.

harmony (p. 46)   Two or more different tones sounding at the same time.

introduction (p. 8)   In a song, music played before the singing begins.

leap (p. 38)   To move from one tone to another, skipping over the tones in between.

lullaby (p. 184)   A quiet song, often sung when rocking a child to sleep.

measure (p. 23)   A grouping of beats set off by bar lines.

melody (p. 32)   A line of single tones that move upward, downward, or repeat.

melody pattern (p. 46)   An arrangement of pitches into a small grouping, usually occurring often in a piece.

meter (p. 22) The way the beats of music are grouped, often in sets of two or in sets of three.

mood (p. 68)   The feeling that a piece of music gives. The *mood* of a lullaby is quiet and gentle.

orchestra (p. 122)   A balanced group of instruments consisting of strings, woodwinds, brass, and percussion.

ostinato (p. 46)   A rhythm or melody pattern that repeats.

partner songs (p. 50)   Two or more different songs that can be sung at the same time to create harmony.

percussion (p. 128)   A group of pitched or unpitched instruments that are played by striking with mallets, beaters, and so on, or by shaking.

phrase (p. 58)   A musical "sentence." Each *phrase* expresses one thought.

refrain (p. 6)   The part of a song that repeats, using the same melody and words.

repeated tones (p. 35)   Two or more tones in a row that have the same sound.

rests (p. 13)   Symbols for silences.

rhythm pattern (p. 87)   A group of long and short sounds. Some rhythm patterns have even sounds. Others have uneven sounds.

rondo (p. 80)   A musical form in which a section is repeated, with contrasting sections in between (such as ABACA).

round (p. 53)   A follow-the-leader process in which all sing the same melody but start at different times.

sequence (p. 64)   The repetition of a melody pattern at a higher or lower pitch level.

shanties (p. 156)   Sailors' work songs.

solo (p. 98)   Music for a single singer or player, often with an accompaniment.

steady beat (p. 12)   Regular pulses.

step (p. 38)   To move from one tone to another without skipping tones in between.

strings (p. 124)   A term used to refer to stringed instruments that are played by bowing, plucking, or strumming.

strong beat (p. 286)   The first beat in a measure.

suite (p. 163)   An instrumental work of several movements, often programmatic or descriptive.

tempo (p. 66)   The speed of the beat in music.

theme (p. 56)   An important melody that occurs several times in a piece of music.

tone color (p. 96)   The special sound that makes one instrument or voice sound different from another.

trio (p. 104)   Any composition for three voices or instruments, each having a separate part.

variation (p. 94)   Music that is repeated but changed in some important way.

woodwinds (p. 125)   A term used to refer to wind instruments, now or originally made of wood.

CLASSIFIED INDEX

FOLK, TRADITIONAL, AND REGIONAL

POETRY AND STORIES

RECORDED INTERVIEWS

Careers in Music

THEME MUSICAL: EARTH DAY

SONG INDEX

Acknowledgments and Picture Credits

Acknowledgments

Credit and appreciation are due publishers and copyright owners for the use of the following:

"Clear Evening After Rain" from ONE HUNDRED POEMS FROM THE CHINESE by Kenneth Rexforth. © 1971 by Kenneth Rexforth. All rights reserved. Used by permission New Directions Publishing Corporation. Four African Proverbs from AFRICAN PROVERBS compiled by Charlotte and Wolf Leslau. © 1962 (copyright renewed) by Peter Pauper Press. Used by permission. "Grandfather Frog" from ANOTHER HERE AND NOW STORY BOOK by Lucy Sprague Mitchell. Copyright 1937 by E. P. Dutton, renewed © 1965 by Lucy Sprague Mitchell. Used by permission of Dutton Children's Books, a division of Penguin Books USA Inc. "Hallowe'en" from THE LITTLE HILL, Poems & Pictures by Harry Behn. © 1949 by Harry Behn. Copyright renewed 1977 by Alice L. Behn. Reprinted by permission of Marion Reiner. "I Am Crying from Thirst" from THE WHISPERING WIND by Alonzo Lopez. Used by permission of the author. "Noonday Sun" from COWBOYS AND INDIANS by Kathryn & Byron Jackson. © 1968, 1948 Western Publishing Company. Used by permission. "The Little Shekere," Words and Music by Nitanju Bolade Casel. Clear Ice Music. Used by permission.

Every effort has been made to locate all copyright holders of material used in this book. If any errors or omissions have occurred, corrections will be made.

Photograph and Illustration Credits

All photographs are by Silver Burdett Ginn (SBG) unless otherwise noted.

Cover: Bernard Bonhomme.
2: Lisa Pomerantz. 6–7: Steven Mach. 8–9: Blake Thorton; *inset* Michael Ochs Archives. 10–11: Richard A. Green/Rags Photography. 14–15: SuperStock. 16–17: *title and background ill.* Mark Smith; 16: *inset* Mark Mueller. 20–21: Jennifer Hewittson. 22–23: Elliott Erwitt/Magnum. 26–27: Bettmann Archives. 26: *t.* Michael Ochs Archives. 27: *b.* Bettmann Archives. 28–29: Dorthea Sierra. 30–31: John Guider/International Stock Photo; *inset* North Wind Picture Archives. 30: *b.* North Wind Picture Archives. 34–35: Benton Mahon. 36–39: Cheryl Chalmers. 42: Elliot Smith for SBG. 44–45: Cathy Diefendorf. 46–47: Andrea Eberbach. 48–49: Francisco Mora. 50–51: Liz Conrad. 52–53: Elliot Smith for SBG. 56–57: *ill.* Jeffery Terreson; *photograph b.* Archives Larousse-Giraudon/Art Resource. 59: *b.* Courtesy of Elizabeth Catlett. 60–61: Andrea Eberbach. 62–63: *ill.* Blake Thorton; *insets* Michael Ochs Archives. 65: Roy Morsch/The Stock Market. 66–67: Rene David Michael; *inset* Bettmann Archives. 68–69: Deborah Healey; *inset* Culver Pictures. 72–73: Benjamin Vincent. 74–75: Stephen Studd/Tony Stone Images; *inset* Culver Pictures. 76: Culver Pictures. 78–79: Frank Daniel; *inset* Elliott Smith for SBG. 80–81: Rhonda Voo. 84: Joe Veno. 88: John Running. 89: Jerry Jacka Photography. 91: Arthur Tress/Magnum. 92–93: Caryn King. 94–95: Jeffery Terreson. 96–97: John Berg. 98–99: *inset* Frank Rossotto/The Stock Market. 100–101: Kathleen Kinkopf. 103: Elliot Smith for SBG. 104-105: *t., m.* Elliott Smith for SBG. 108-109: BMI/Michael Ochs Archives. 110–111: Blake Thorton. 112-113: Superstock; *insets t.* © John Serrao/Photo Researchers, Inc.; *b.l.* © S.R. Maglione/Photo Researchers, Inc.; *b.r.* Picture Perfect. 114–115: © A.B. Joyce/Photo Researchers, Inc. 116–117: Donna Ingemonson. 118–119: Archive Photos. 120: Kirk Schlea/Picture Perfect. 122–123: Four by Five/SuperStock. 128: Bettmann Archives. 132: Burton Morris. 134–135: Victor Vaccaro. 136–137: Tom Tonkin. 138: David FeBland. 140–141: *ill.* Rick Farrell; *background.* Archive Photos. 143: David Diaz; *inset* Archive Photos. 144-145: W. Hille/Leo deWys, Inc. 147: D. D. Bryant. 148; Blake Thornton. 149: Elliott Smith for SBG. 150–151: Mike Reed. 152–153: Pamela Harrelson. 154–155: *ill.* Olivia Cole. 156; *inset* Culver Pictures. 157: Gwen Connelly. 158–159: *ill.* Blake Thorton; *photogragh* © C. Seghers/Photo Researchers, Inc. 160–161: Kelly Hume. 162-163: Joanne Lotter/TOM STACK & ASSOCIATES. 164–165: Kelly Hume. 166–167: Vincent Caputo. 168–169: David Slonim. 170–171: Blake Thorton. 172-173: Jacki Gelb. 174–175: *ill.* Joyce Protzman; *photographs t.m.* Bill Holden/Leo deWys, Inc.; *t.r.* The Image Works; *m.l.* Anthony Cassidy/Tony Stone Images; *m.r.* SuperStock; *b.* Karen McCunnall/Leo deWys, Inc. *b.r.* Steve Vidler/Leo deWys, Inc. 176–177: Holly Bogdanffy. 181: *t.l.* Gerard Lacz/Animals, Animals; *t.m.* Stephen Dalton/Animals, Animals; *t.r.* J.L. Stevenson/Animals, Animals; *b.l.* Robert Maier/Animals, Animals; *b.m.* Jack Griffin/Animals, Animals; *b.r.* Oxford Scientific Films/Animals, Animals. 182–183: Fridmar Damm/Leo de Wys, Inc.: *inset* Fridmar Damm/Leo deWys, Inc. 184–185: *ill.* Iskra Johnson; *photography* SuperStock; *inset* The Image Works; . 186–187: Kumiko Robinson; *inset* Four by Five/SuperStock. 188: *t.* Peter Baker/Leo deWys, Inc.; *b.l.* J. Eigen/Leo deWys, Inc. 190: Iskra Johnson. 191: Geoffrey Hiller/Leo deWys, Inc. 194-195: © Ben Schneider/Photo Researchers, Inc.; *inset* Brown Brothers. 198: *.l* Bob Daemmrich/Stock, Boston. 200–201: Len Berger/Picture Perfect. 202–203: Joann Adinolfi. 204–205: Culver Pictures. 206–209: Joe Boddy. 210-211: Jerry Pavey. 212–213: Steve Solum/Bruce Coleman, Inc. 215: Berenholtz/The Stock Market. 216–219: Eva Cockville. 218-219: *photographs* Robert Frerck/Odyssey Productions. 220-221: Suzanne L. Murphy/D.D. Bryant; *ill.* Cathy Diefendorf. 223: Collections/Brian Shuel. 226–227: *ill.* Mark Mueller; *inset* Suzanne L. Murphy/D.D. Bryant. 228: Lawrence Migdale. 230–231: Jackie Geyer. 232–239: Deborah Pinkney. 240: Roger Huyssen. 242–243: *ill.* Cathy Diefendorf; *photograph* Paul Barton/The Stock Market. 244–245: R.P. Falls/Bruce Coleman, Inc. 246–247: Lili Robins. 248–249: E.R. Degginger/Animals, Animals. 251: Sally Schaedler; *border* Bob Dacey. 252–253: Ken Graham/Bruce Coleman, Inc.; *insets* Johnny Johnson/Animals, Animals. 254: Cathy O'Conner. 255: Larry Winborg. 257: Gary Colby. 259: Liisa Chauncy Guida. 261: Liisa Chauncy Guida. 262: C. C. Lockwood/Earth Scenes; *ill.* Mark Mueller. 263: J. Eastcott/Earth Scenes. 264: Rob McDougal. 266: SuperStock. 267: Cathy Diefendorf. 269: © Vanessa Vick/Photo Researchers, Inc. 270: Victor Engelbert/Picture Perfect. 271: Denise Infernando. 272: SuperStock. 273: Carol Newsom. 275: *ill.* Cathy O'Conner. 276: *ill.* Daphne Hewitt; *photograph* Sally Lightfoot/Bruce Coleman. 277: Cathy O'Conner. 280: *ill.* Joe Taylor; *photograph* Jane Burton/Bruce Coleman. 281: William Maughn. 282: Jeff Gnass/The Stock Market. 283: Rob MacDougal. 284: Picture Perfect. 289: Steven Dalton/Animals, Animals. 290: Elliott Smith for SBG. 292: Jeffery Terreson. 293: Luis Villota/The Stock Market. 295: Liisa Chauncy Guida. 299: Mark Smith. 301: Bob Dacey. 302–303: Ed Simpson/Tony Stone Images; *inset* Courtesy of George Pickow.

Sound Bank Photos 306: *Arpa-* Bill Albrecht for SBG. 307: *Native American Flute-* The Shrine to Music Museum/University of South Dakota. 308: *Oud-* The Shrine to Music Museum/University of South Dakota; *Requinto-* Courtesy of Zazhil/Bill Albrecht for SBG; *Sitar-* The Shrine to Music Museum/University of South Dakota; *Tabla-* The Shrine to Music Museum/University of South Dakota.

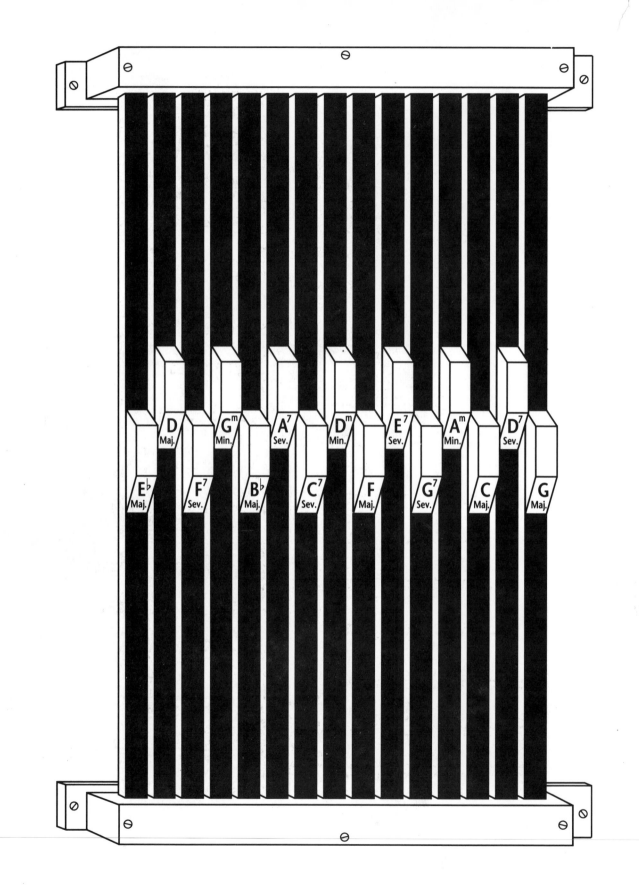